The COLLAPSE of AN AMERICAN FAMILY

Kevin Bassoon

authorHOUSE®

AuthorHouse™
1663 Liberty Drive, Suite 200
Bloomington, IN 47403
www.authorhouse.com
Phone: 1-800-839-8640

First published by AuthorHouse   8/11/2008

ISBN: 978-1-4389-0664-5 (sc)

Printed in the United States of America
Bloomington, Indiana
This book is printed on acid-free paper.

CONTENTS

CHAPTER 1

In the Beginning

It was August of 2005 when I experienced firsthand the decay of our moral fiber in America. I live in a small south Oklahoma town called Shawnee, approximately 20 miles north of Oklahoma City. The town itself has about 40,000 people in it and everybody knows everybody. This close knit community has been a blessing to my family and as you're going to find out has also been a double-edged sword.

I thought if anybody amongst our friends and family had "the ultimate all-American family" that it was our home. My wife and I had been married for twenty-two years, we had already seen our beloved son walk across the stage as a graduate and our 2 lovely daughters were superior athletes with honor roll averages in school. What more could you ask for?

The truth was that our daughters had some dirty little secrets that only they and few others were privy to. These secrets were about to be uncovered and blow up in our home and family like an "atom bomb" of unparallel destruction that we had not heretofore experienced. The casualties would be severe, and the wounds would be deep, very deep!

My wife and I have served the children in our community for over ten years. We have assisted in local churches serving in the capacity of children's coordinators, whereby we organized volunteers for church services, camps, vacation bible schools and a whole lot more. We have helped in our community by volunteering our time in local schools. Whether it was running the school store when our children were in sixth grade or bringing free lunches to children to show we cared, not only for our kids but for the whole community. I know beyond a shadow of a doubt that Sarah and I gave our very heart and soul to KIDS.

Would our very own daughters take advantage of such a fairy tale life? Would they conspire together against us? And would other dysfunctional families step in and defend our daughters' dirty little secrets? We shall see, we shall see.

It was early on a Sunday morning when I heard a knock on the bedroom door. "Who is it?" I inquired. "It's Sabrina." I told Sabrina to open the door and come on in. She knows I love my back scratched. For years I would demand the girls to scratch my back when I got home from work. It finally got to the point that when I would yell to have one of the girls scratch my back that they would both make a run for it and hide as fast as they could. I can still hear their footsteps running out of the living room when they would hear the dreaded words, "Ellen, Sabrina can I see you for a moment."

So Sabrina walks into my bedroom and begins for the first time to willingly scratch my back and says "Daddy, you're the best Dad in the whole world, you always let me go to my friends' house when I ask, and I'm only 15 and you've allowed me to go to Oklahoma City, Muskogee, and Tulsa with my boyfriend and his Dad." Sabrina had prefaced her question with astounding words of approval for her sweet, thoughtful, caring father. She then asked me the question that would begin the land slide of deception and betrayal. "Daddy, my good friend Hillary called and asked if I could go spend the day with her?" My reply as a trusting father was, "You bet ya Hot Shot" and Sabrina, I said, "Do one thing for me?" She said, "Anything for the Number One Dad in America." "Sabrina make it a great day!"

As I was lying on the most comfortable bed in the world , Sabrina called from her cell phone not 2 minutes after she had left my room. I answered the phone and Sabrina said "Dad, what was I thinking? I always hug you before I leave and tell you I love you. Hillary's already picked me up and I just wanted to re-emphasize how much I love you." I left her with these words, "I love you more, have a good one."

My youngest daughter, Sabrina, was living a double life and deceiving her mother and me for a long time. She was abusing our love and trust in ways that we couldn't imagine. At fifteen years old Sabrina was already involved in very promiscuous behavior which involved lying and manipulating others, sexual misconduct, sneaking out of our safe home, and many other things that are too painful to mention.

Why would she do this? What was causing her to need more attention than we already gave her? Was she hormonally imbalanced, or temporarily chemically out of whack? If we knew then what we now know we would have braced ourselves for what was just ahead. Sabrina's behavior was about to be completely exposed and her plots uncovered. This would all lead to the dreaded counter attack by Sabrina against our family. THE SKILL in which Sabrina would begin to pick us apart would be unfathomable. Get ready for some drama and confusion stirred up by one little girls desire to justify herself, even at her beloved family's expense!

On this particular Sunday morning, my wife, Sarah was serving at a local church as the nursery director. When she arrived home I told her that our sweet little angel Sabrina was at Hillary's house. She handed off the baton to me and off I went to work in Muskogee, a city twenty miles north of Shawnee. Oh, the hours of work we put in to see that our kids have the very best!

When I came home on that fateful night I was very tired from working the previous seven days in a row. As I walked through the door Sarah came up to me and uttered these words in my ear, "I love you big boy, thanks for working for the team." That's the kind of girl I married over two decades ago. A woman who works hard, loves her family and is the quintessential giver. If I could sum up my wife's very existence it would be that she lives to give!!

We made some small talk and then asked each other if she or I had heard from Sabrina since she left the house ten hours before. Neither one of us had been called by Sabrina all day long. This was a first. She usually gave us a courtesy call to let us know how her day was going. We decided to call the Miller's house and see how everything was going.

We never expected to confront what we were about to face from our sweet little angel. Have you ever been hit by something when you weren't looking? It was like we were standing on the side of the road and all of a sudden "wham" a car hits you right below the pelvis and the next thing you know is you're doing a nice gymnastic somersault over the hood. Mr. Miller answered our call that day, and said concerning Sabrina being at his house, "We haven't even seen Sabrina all day long." What? Where could she be? Is she all right? Our hearts started beating fast as we said a prayer for the safe return of our beloved daughter. Our prayer must have sounded something like this, "Help us dear God. Help!!"

Immediately after we prayed I had a thought of something that happened three days before with Sabrina. Her mother and I had talked and discussed her relationship with her boyfriend. We were thinking since Sabrina was a mere fifteen years old and Clifford was seventeen maybe it wasn't the best idea for them to be spending so much time together.

As we talked to Sabrina she began to cry, saying, "Mom and Dad, we're just friends, that's all. Please don't take away a good friend!" For Sabrina to be so emotional about this made us think that maybe we had jumped to conclusions about their relationship and that they were really semi-saints. We changed our minds about Sabrina seeing Clifford and told her we were sorry for thinking our little angel could be tempted like the average teenager. (Our kids are above average). Sabrina immediately quit crying and hugged me and Sarah and said, "What did I do to deserve parents as good as you two!"

After I had this thought I told Sarah, "She's with Clifford. I just know it, I darn well know it!" Sarah, always believing the best replied to me, "Kevin, you're letting your mind race. Sabrina wouldn't break the trust in our relationship over one immature boy." Sarah was about to get blindsided worse than me concerning Sabrina and her behavior. Can you say denial? Get ready, Sarah. Your daughter's behind the wheel of a big bus and it's coming right at us!

I called Sabrina's cell phone and there was no answer, just silence. I decided to leave a message stating to Sabrina that I knew who she was with and that as of now she'd lost her cell phone. Immediately, she called back and as I conversed with her I noticed that she was talking in the squeakiest little baby's voice I'd ever heard. It honest to goodness sounded like a two year old who got caught with their hand in the cookie jar. Instead, it was Sabrina getting caught with her hands in Clifford's pants!

Sabrina had now been gone for over 11 hours and was with Clifford, her innocent friend, as she put it. Clifford reminds me of Eddie Haskell from Leave it to Beaver. No matter where I saw him he would always come up and shake my hand and say, "Mr. Bassoon, do you know what

5

an honor it is to date your daughter?" Ouch, Clifford, you're kissing my butt too hard, it's going to leave a hickey!

I don't think Clifford or Sabrina was expecting what was going to happen when they arrived at my home in Clifford's white truck. The same white truck our property manager told me she saw Sabrina and Clifford in having one heck of a time. Sabrina, get ready for your sweet Daddy to put a stop to all this ASAP!

Clifford looked like a cow at a new gate when he noticed my countenance was very disconcerting towards him and Sabrina. I opened his door and released a beautiful synchronized tirade that sounded something like this, "Get the hell off my property and don't plan on seeing my under age daughter again." Clifford showed his true colors and floored his engine, speeding off into the darkness.

Now what should we do with Sabrina? She wasn't talking, and when she did it still resembled that of a toddler. We decided to take her phone from her and ground her for a few days. We surmised that this would be enough to encourage her to change her behavior. But this was just the beginning of birth pains of things yet to come. The "monster" within Sabrina was about to unleash hell itself against our family, the community and the church. Beware friends and family the thief is coming to steal, kill and destroy every relationship possible. Hell hath no fury like a woman scorned!!

Sabrina has always been very stubborn and strong–willed. When she was just a toddler I can still recall my father and mother-in-law telling me and Sarah that they had never seen a more determined child bent on getting her way. Sabrina was in a pickle regarding her deceptive behavior being exposed. What would she do?

Sabrina was about to embark on a personal mission of dividing and conquering all who stood in her path. One of her main weapons of mass destruction was blame shifting. She would have to seek and search with all of her heart someone she could dump her load of guilt on. But who? Who could she target to be her proverbial scapegoat?

Her original father, Adam, would be so proud of her learning his ways. Do you remember when Adam's Father came to him and said, "Did you do what I asked you not to do?" His initial response was the new found art of blame shifting. It's the woman's fault that "You" gave me. Believe me when I say my young teen-age daughter would put Adam to shame with her skills of shifting the blame to another.

Sabrina's first target was her older sister, Ellen. She subtly began to confide every tid bit of information to Ellen concerning her deceptive behavior. Ellen was aware of Sabrina's secret rendezvous with Clifford and loved rescuing her younger sister. Ellen didn't have any social relationship with boys, so she was getting fulfillment through Sabrina's sneaky, covert behavior.

We were well on our way to becoming a house divided. Our daughters were preparing to blow up the foundation of trust and respect that my wife and I had spent two decades building. Sabrina would be the leader and Ellen would station the bombs exactly where Sabrina instructed her to. I can already hear the rumbling of the bridge of trust and respect beginning to crumble.

Sabrina had enlisted Ellen as a sergeant, under her authority and now she sought to bring our beloved older son on board. She was secretly calling my son and painting herself as an abused, poorly treated victim since we took her cell phone from her. Can you imagine the audacity to confiscate Sabrina's cell phone? How was she supposed to call Clifford? How was she supposed to know if he was coming at 3 a.m. or 4 a.m.? Our approval rating from Sabrina was now on the decline.

We, as her parents, had never required anything from her. All we wanted was for her to have a good self-esteem and leave our home in tip top shape, ready to take life by the horns. In hindsight we should have had her clean her room, do the dishes and take out the trash. Because of this, in her mind Mom and Dad were put on this earth to make her happy. She would go and clean other people's houses, but never did she help around our house. Parents, please learn from my mistakes and work your little blessings at the home front so you don't raise a totally narcissistic teenager like we did! How dare we take her cell phone, she must have thought we had really gone overboard.

I want to take a moment and tell you that our daughter's rebellion to such good parents I believe is a direct result of certain attitudes and beliefs we are seeing from Hollywood all the way down to South Oklahoma. We are raising kids to think about themselves first and everyone else last.

There is also a movement that is gaining steam that is totally deteriorating the fabric of the family. It goes like this, real men are those who are in touch with their feminine side and to be a man you should be more sensitive, more tactful, and basically act more like a woman.

I can see Rosie O'Donnell and Oprah holding up a big pair of scissors to our male genetalia and saying, "A few more snips and all of them will be geldings!" It's trickling all the way down to southern Oklahoma. Beware of the scissors in your area. (Theme music of the twilight zone playing).

You will see in the coming chapters that I know firsthand about the dreaded scissors all too well. You will see how our close knit community hindered our family's recovery process and fueled the flame for more rebellion from our destructive daughter. Last but not least you will see how a pastor gave the worst counsel of all! Read on and learn from your fellow gelding.

CHAPTER 2

The All American Family?

Being a parent is on the job training. Would you parents say a hearty amen to that? My wife and I wanted to be as prepared as possible when the day came for us to have the responsibility of being a Mom and a Dad. That is why we went to a two year school and majored in children's education. We learned some valuable life lessons from men and women who had already gone down the road before us as loving parents.

I distinctly remember one of my favorite instructors, Dr. Carter, teaching a lesson on parenting. The title of his teaching said it all. Parenting, pain or pleasure? Both! Oh how true it would be for me in the coming years to remember that phrase. Our family had experienced heaven on earth for nearly two decades, but the pain was right around the corner.

When our beautiful children were in their infancy years Sarah and I, along with adoring friends and relatives showered our children abundantly with non-stop love and approval. Our lives in many ways centered on blessing our kids with the world's best childhood. This was a huge goal for Sarah and me, and one that we thoroughly enjoyed.

I was my son's baseball and basketball coach during his formative years. We enrolled the girls in soccer and community and church activities on a weekly basis. Looking back I would have to say that our home was like a dream on Fantasy Island. It was that good. I can see me and my family getting off the plane and Tattoo greeting us, "Welcome to Fantasy Island where all of your dreams come true!"

The most fun we ever had as a family was take vacations together. Sometimes it was going with our good friends, Van and Kristy to the beach where we fished together, ate together or went sightseeing. We had some awesome times. Sarah used to take the girls by themselves to different cities to just shop and hang out . They always came back refreshed and full of joy! (Oh the good old days). Can you hear the song playing, "Yesterday, life was such an easy game to play, oh I believe in yesterday…." Let's don't get too nostalgic.

My wife's favorite time of year was without a shadow of a doubt Christmas. She would secretly shop and hide gifts for all of us, and surprise us with such acts of kindness. Her favorite thing was the "stocking stuffers". We each received a boat load of items that Sarah individually picked out just for us, the most special people in her life. Thanks honey, for being the biggest giver I've ever met . You complete me!

What the heck happened to such a fairy tale home? How could two teen-age girls who'd become drama queens destroy the firm foundation we spent two decades building? Did they have some help from a few adults that usurped our authority? Read on my friend and you'll be amazed at the plots and plans that attacked our American family.

Sabrina had been caught in her deceitfulness, reprimanded and grounded for her selfish, manipulative behavior. Although my wife and I hated disciplining Sabrina, we knew we had to make an attempt to bridle our newfound wild horse. (Whoo, was she bucking?) Watch out honey, I think she's going to kick you and me right in the noggin.

10

Looking back we should have checked Sabrina out to see if she had a chemical imbalance, or was it hormonal? Her behavior changed oh so quickly. Maybe it was drugs? I don't know that we'll ever know why she did what she did, but hopefully anyone who reads this book will learn from our mistakes and raise healthy, productive citizens that care more for others than themselves.

I had taken educational psychology at Texas A&M, but I was not prepared for what Sabrina was about to put our family through. She was about to get a full head of steam and huff and puff and try to blow our house down.

After we took Sabrina's cell phone, she began to take her manipulative game to a higher level. She began to tell these outrageous stories of her rescuing others who were in dire need. I distinctly remember coming home from work two days after we caught Sabrina in her web of deception and being amazed at what was transpiring in my living room.

My wife was in tears as she relayed to me the amazing, spectacular story of what Sabrina did for a fellow classmate at school. Sarah began by telling me, "Kevin, listen to what our sweet daughter did at school today in the midst of her trying time?" Sabrina with tears also rushing down her pretty face could hardly get the words out as she said, "Dad, today at school there was a new boy sitting all alone and I couldn't just sit where I was with all the popular kids and watch him eat in solitude. I invited him to sit with us at the popular table."

This is when I first saw Sabrina's gift in full operation. She was able to seduce with enticing words her very own mother in to thinking she had turned into a "Saint". I wasn't falling for our fifteen year old's Mother Theresa imitation. Sabrina was trying to suck my wife into her vacuum called "emotional manipulation". This would be the beginning of my daughter using her talents, skills, and teen-age drama to seduce, deceive and infect people with her destructive newfound "gift".

Later that night I talked to my gullible bride about how Sabrina was using evil communication patterns to seduce her. Sarah understood and would try to be more watchful in the future when Sabrina throws out the bait of "rescuing others" not to chomp down and run with it. Believe me Sabrina was getting ready to throw the bait out to a whole lot more people!

Are you ready to get into the juicy details of this compelling true story? Fasten your seat belts because you're about to go on the ride of your life (weeee!!)

That Thursday my wife and I decided to give Sabrina back her cell phone, and to reaffirm our love for her, in spite of what was going on we were hoping that this was just an isolated instance and we could go back to being that All American Family. We approached Sabrina to tell her the good news of returning her cell phone to her. She was playing on the computer as we handed her back the cell phone and told her, "We love you." She stood up and said, "I think I'm going to pee in my pants, I'm so excited. Ya'll are the very best parents in the whole world!" Would this be the end of the saga? Could we just get back to enjoying the remaining three and half years that Sabrina would be in our home?

On that Sunday night, for some reason, I couldn't sleep and I always sleep like a baby.

I didn't want to wake Sarah up since she was sleeping so sweetly. I went into the living room and fell into a frothing at the mouth deep sleep.

Then suddenly I heard a pounding on my front door at 5 a.m. Who could it be? What the helicopter is going on? As I peered out the door I was shocked to see my youngest daughter in the custody of the Shawnee Police Department. This was the first time an armed officer ever had to step foot on my lawn. Sabrina had that familiar baby face look that says, "How can I paint myself as the victim?" She was dressed with heavy make up and no bra and resembled a 22 year old hooker.

I opened the door as my shock and disbelief was turning to anger as fast as you can say Ticonderoga. (That's a line from the Three Stooges if you didn't know). The officer informed me that our neighbors thought someone was breaking into my house as Sabrina's supposedly ex-boyfriend was helping her out the window and into the safety of his caring arms of lust.

The officer informed me that Sabrina seemed to be good at the skillful art of blame shifting. The very observant officer told me that as she was taking Sabrina to our front door that she began to deflect all the attention off of her own actions and to place them squarely upon her "Father". Can you believe it? She whispered ever so subtly to the officer, "Please don't tell my Dad because he'll hit me."

When the officer told me this I was pissed off that I was Sabrina's new scapegoat. I promptly told Sabrina to get the hell in the house and go to her room. The "monster" within Sabrina was learning how to use the victim card and betray her very own "All American Dad".

I walked outside with the officer and filed criminal trespass charges against Clifford Jones. Clifford is from a broken home and he and Sabrina were two pees in a pod of narcissism. I can hear them singing a duet. It goes something like this "It's all about me, oh it's all about me".

The next day we took Sabrina to school and this is where she began laying the foundation for her master plan to steal, kill and destroy from her loving family. She pulled her paint brush out and started painting a new portrait of our family as dysfunctional. Beware, New Rutherford High School the monster within Sabrina is about to attack all healthy relationships we spent years building. Sabrina was using the victim card as a sledge hammer to slowly erode the trust and security our home had been built upon. (Whack, whack).

This story is about to take some twists and turns involving friends, teachers, administrators, child protective services and some real gullible and meddling acquaintances. Sabrina is about to assemble her team that will further assist her in what I call "Operation Division".

CHAPTER 3

Ground Zero

The next morning after we had taken Ellen and Sabrina to school Sarah and I were shell shocked to find out, not only what Sabrina was doing but that her older sister had known for some time that Sabrina was lying to us, deceiving us and having illicit rendezvous with Clifford Jones.

Ellen, a National Honor Society student and tender hearted and caring sister was enabling her sister to continue her downward spiral. What if Ellen would have had the courage at this point to say to her troubled, beguiling sister, "Stop it, you're heading down a crooked path?" Why couldn't Ellen muster the courage to confront her sister and speak the truth in love to her?

Good question and I think I have the answer. Unbeknownst to me, Ellen and Sabrina didn't view themselves as individuals with separate gifts and talents but as one co–dependant unit. Webster's describes codependency as a psychological condition or a relationship in which a person is controlled or manipulated by another who is affected with a pathological condition.

Sabrina had problems with her emotions and was acting out her inward rebellion in destructive ways (to herself and all of us). Ellen enjoyed rescuing Sabrina; it made her feel involved and useful. They were a team like peanut butter and jelly, like baseball and apple pie, like Bonnie and Clyde, etc....

You are going to find out how destructive this type of a relationship can be. You will see how Sabrina would gravitate like a magnet to codependent rescuers like Ellen and form alliances against her parents that will cross cultural, ethnic and religious boundaries.

The next morning when we dropped Sabrina off at school is when she began to take "Operation Division" to a ground zero level. She was in a quandary, either she would repent for lying, manipulating, sneaking out, etc. or she would bow her back like a two by four and release an all out blitzkrieg attack against her all American parents. You guessed it right. The wrath and fury of our little angel was being kindled and aimed right at her loving parents.

Sabrina pulled out the victim card that was so useful in past confrontations and began describing to her friends how tough her life had become since she was caught with her hand in the cookie jar. Some of her friends, who I've known for years, started coming up to me at sporting events and asking me if I really had the temper that Sabrina said she saw on display with Clifford and when the armed officers escorted her home.

Was I being set up by my own daughter? Was she willing to stop at nothing until THE AUTHORITY figure in her life was dead by character assassination. The monster within Sabrina would not cease and desist its operations until I compelled it to. Would I give in to the domination of my fifteen year old daughter? Would I quit being her father and back the hell up? The answer is hell no. No matter if my daughter felt empowered by her older sister, her friends, and any other rescuers I would not allow her scissors to make me into a gelding in my own home!

That next weekend was a volleyball tournament, so as always I went up to the school to support our teams. My wife is a part-time volleyball ref and she was already at the gym when I arrived. I went over and gave her a hug and we made some small talk before she had to resume referring the games.

This is the point when I knew Sabrina was drawing many other people into her web of deception. One of our neighbor's daughters came up to me and said, "Mr. Bassoon I've never seen you angry in all these years I've known you. But your own daughter said you are releasing psychotic anger towards her and she's getting afraid." I didn't have on my bullet proof vest, so I got hit by one of Sabrina's messengers. (boom) Sabrina was strapping mini bombs on her friends and having them come up to me and discharge her evil weapons. (wham)

When I saw Sabrina she was smiling and putting on a façade of acceptable behavior. She came up to me and gave me a kiss in between games and immediately I had the thought of a quote I memorized many years before. It says, "Faithful are the wounds of a friend but deceitful are the kisses of an enemy."

When I returned from work that night I came into the house and decided to take my daughter on a little drive that she would never forget. What was about to happen would be ammunition in Sabrina's arsenal that she would draw upon to demonize me and paint herself as THE VICTIM.

I drove her to the grocery store and parked the car. I turned off the engine and in no uncertain terms demanded Sabrina to quit firing the bombs at me and her mother! I said, "Stop the crap and get your d... scissors away from my balls!!" She, leaned forward and said in a deep voice, "I don't know what you're talking about, how am I supposed to stop Ellen or others from rescuing me?" That's what Sabrina thinks love is, if you rescue her. I raised my voice and finally got the wild bronco temporarily tamed. I drew a line in the sand and warned her to never cross it again!!!!!!!

By losing my temper with Sabrina I had given her another bullet in her gun and believe me she was about to fire her best shot thus far. But she, as a codependent, would rather do her dirty work through someone else. But who could she get to fire her weapons of mass destruction? Watch out Sarah, Ellen, Michael and all of our friends? The beast within Sabrina is about to be completely released from her cage. I am woman watch me roar!

Get ready for more twists and turns than a NASCAR race. Fasten your seat belts. The real juicy stuff is almost here. It will blow your mind how a loving American Dad is about to be castrated by a community, friends and family!!!!!!!!

CHAPTER 4

Are We Changing
as a Society for the Better?

Let's regress for a moment and take a look back in the rear view mirror and see some of the changes we've made in the last 40 years in America and see if we're changing for the better or for the worse. Could any of the factors I'm getting ready to talk about have an influence on our young people? Like my daughter, Sabrina?

Let's take a look at Hollywood and their impressionable influence on our American culture. Let me list to you some of the top rated movies of the 60's, 70's and of today and you tell me if the family is better represented then or now. Here are some of the top rated shows of the 60's: Gun Smoke, Wagon Train, Andy Griffith, The Jack Benny Show, and My Three Sons.

How about the 70's: Marcus Welby, M.D., Beretta, Bonanza, Adam 12 and Flip Wilson were some of the highest rated shows. Let's look at some the top rated shows today: Jerry Springer, Maury, Beauty and the Geek, Oprah, and let's not forget the drama of Desperate Housewives.

You be your own judge if you think T.V. has gone from a fun, entertaining, family type environment to smut! Are the images that our young people are seeing affecting them in positive ways? When they see men acting like women (Queer Eye For the Straight Guy) and women acting like men (Rosie "testosterone" O'Donnell), does that give them a true image of what society should be like? Yea, if you want to live in France with the rest of the geldings!

This is America, the Land of the Free and the Home of the Brave! Our forefathers stood up regardless of popular opinion and gave us hope of a better tomorrow and we're slowly chopping at the foundation of what they gave their lives to build, just as my daughters have been chopping at our family foundation for the last year and a half.

Can we peer back into our political past and see some changes. And if so, are they for the better or for the worse? You are the judge? Let's look at the Democratic Party in the last forty years. I'm thinking of one of our past presidents John F. Kennedy. The statement that I'll always remember him saying was "Ask not what your country can do for you, but ask what you can do for your country." That phrase has been embedded in my mind since I took History in Junior High school.

Let's roll forward to Bill Clinton and look at his most famous statement that our young kids remember. President Clinton will forever be remembered for these words, "It depends what the meaning of the word is, is." Bill was referring to his scandalous encounter with Monica Lewinsky, or was it Janet Reno he was with. (No, that's who Hillary was with in the other room).

No, our American politics has changed dramatically; and not for the better. But could all this be trickling down all the way to southern Oklahoma and influencing our young people and even my daughters? You bet ya, cowboys and cowgirls!

Let's look at lawsuits and the legal system. Are we in a better place of bringing truth and justice into the country? Does anybody remember the OJ trial? We all know he butchered two innocent souls and about decapitated his children's mother. Yet truth and justice was not served for the Brown or Goldman family.

What was the result of this hideous decision in Los Angeles? They had a dadgum victory parade celebrating OJ's aquittal. Can you see Jesse (I Hate Caucasions) Jackson and Rev Al Sharpton leading the march with uplifted hands praising God for the death of two innocent Americans. How were the Goldman and Brown families feeling as the murder march began? Do you think they trust our court system? What did that trial say? It said right is wrong and wrong is right.

Now you have people suing McDonalds because their coffee is served hot and fresh. McDonalds actually has to put a warning on their coffee that tells dummies that coffee is hot. What about lawsuits against tobacco companies? They're being raked over the coals because cigarettes are bad for you. No duh Sherlock. Who made you drive down to the store, open up your car door, walk into the store and purchase an item, light the end of it with fire and suck it into your lungs? Does that sound like my daughter's victim mentality? You're kidding me if you don't think our young people are picking up on our poor little woe is me attitude in America.

What would our courageous forefathers think of us now? If our World War I and World War II veterans that shed their blood for us were to come back today, would they think we've made progress? Can you imagine what they'd think if they flipped on the TV and saw two men sucking each others face and saying they deserve special rights because of their sexual preference? What would they think of Rosie bashing Donald Trump and Tom Selleck for having balls bigger than hers?

Can you see Rosie, Oprah, and Hilary all holding up their gelding scissors and roaring like lions for all men to line up and "take it like a man" as they emasculate every last one of us from sea to shining sea. Beware my brothers in whatever state of the union you live. If it happened to me it can happen to you!

I think too many of us in America are concerned with our approval rating and therefore are afraid to stand up and say right is right and wrong is wrong. I know personally from the opposition I faced while trying to curb my bucking little bronco, Sabrina, that we've got some opposition aligned against the structure of the family. I for one, as you will see later in this book, will not be moved through the art of manipulation or codependent rescuing.

I believe that there can be no lasting positive change without the ability to leave the status quo and shout from the housetops, "Come hell or high water, I will not be moved!" Let's look at some people who went against the grain and had a positive impact on the society in which they lived.

First of all, let's look at Martin L. King and the influence he's had on our society. He said he had a dream that people wouldn't be judged by the color of their skin, but by their actions. Forty years ago I can promise you his message was not popular, and yet what he said was the truth. His approval rating was so low by certain sects of society that he was martyred for his beliefs. But look at how his life has affected our country for positive change. I dare say that if there had not been a Martin L. King then Tony Dungy wouldn't have been holding the Lombardi trophy as the first African American head coach to win a Super Bowl! We're making great strides regarding race in our country in spite of the rainbow coalition trying to drag us all back to the 60's. We all understand that Jesse Jackson wouldn't have a job if he couldn't find somebody to rescue. (other than African Americans)

Is the majority always right? What about our brothers at the Alamo that made a stand against the Mexican army. They only had a handful of men, but they believed so much in their mission that they gave their very lives for the cause! If they hadn't died for us, then I dare say in south Texas, Texans would be saying "no hablo engles" instead of being a part of the greatest country on earth.

What is my point? I'm glad you asked. The point is that we don't have to agree with the people that are attacking the moral fiber of America, the family. There should be one Mom and one Dad as the governing authorities in the home and society should respect the parent's role as overseers, even if a family has a child like mine, hell bent on attacking her own home like a heat seeking missile! Let's quit empowering our kids by rescuing them because we've had a few cases of abuse and let's get behind Mom and Dad and show some support! Let's get honor back in the schools that left when prayer was taken out. Let's demand honor back in our homes. We can do it!!!!!!!!

CHAPTER 5

From Functional to Dysfunctional in a Day

My son, Michael, and I have had the closest relationship I've ever seen between a father and his son. Besides being his basketball and baseball coach I was also his children's church director from the time he was six until he was twelve years old. Every Thursday night for years we'd go to a Christian boy scouts organization called "Rhema Rangers". After I closed down the building and locked everything up we'd always stop by the store and get a drink and a snack for our ride home together.

As Michael grew older and moved out of our house there was a natural progression of re- stablishing boundaries in the relationship. He was turning into a man and was deciding who and what he wanted to be for his own life. And we, as his parents were changing in our dealing with him not the boy he once was bot as a man. How many of you older parents know what I'm talking about?

This normal change in the relationship was occurring right at the same time Sabrina's estrogen was kicking in and exhibiting her rebellious, narcisstic behavior. Would she seize the moment and try to recruit Michael to rescue her like Ellen already was doing? Would she capitalize on the opportune moment and try to incorporate more people on her team of Operation Division?

Sabrina began secretly calling my beloved son, Michael and setting him up, like she did her friends at school, to carry some of her destructive grenades of hate and division. She wouldn't have to take responsibility for her feelings of anger. She could work through other innocent people to steal, kill and destroy any relationship she could. Co-dependant people are some of the smartest people on the earth!!

Let's eavesdrop on one of Sabrina's calls. She waits until I leave the house and dials his number. While the phone's ringing she peeks outside to make sure the big bad wolf, formerly known as the all American Dad isn't coming. She sees that the coast is clear and begins talking with one of her subjects, my dear son.

Michael picks up the phone and says, " Hello, Sabrina, what's up?" Sabrina begins her diatribe that sounds something like this. "Mike, I know you've had a great relationship with Dad for all these years but, have you noticed Dad being angry more than he use to be?" Mike responds, "Not really, but what's going on?" Sabrina slowly throws out the bait to Michael and is hoping through her cunningness he'll take it and run with it and be empowered by her to agree together against "THE DAD".

Michael mentions to his baby sister who was talking in her newfound toddler voice that one time in 18 years of living at the house that I got angry with him. I don't know about any of you out there who have reared three kids over two decades and to have only gotten really angry at your oldest one time. I think that's pretty darn good. What do you think?

As soon as Michael mentioned that he had once experienced my wrath, Sabrina had some more ammunition in her gun of deception that she could fire at the opportune time. She promptly hung up the phone after sneakily setting Michael up for her future use. Michael thought his relationship with his sister was private; he had no clue that Sabrina's co-dependant personality was just using him like a druggy uses a syringe to inject the poison into their system.

Sabrina was just about ready to launch her strategic strike into the very heart and core of the family. She now had enough information to create a diversionary tactic that would once and for all take the attention off her own actions and create a "smoking gun" whereby all of us would be tangled in her web of destruction. Watch out Sarah, Sabrina, our sweet youngest daughter will stop at nothing until you my darling dear are also on her team of rescuing. It's good that Sabrina has, in her mind, Michael and Ellen, but if somehow she could get her mother to join the rescuing team, that would really justify her and create the utmost diversionary tactic!!

Sabrina knew that to get my wife who's lived with me for over twenty years to rescue her she would have to plant a seed of doubt concerning my behavior. This girl is smart. She would use her mother's maternal love against her own husband. Sabrina was lighting the fuse to "her bomb" in our living room and slowly backing up and letting all of us walk right into her PATH OF DESTRUCTION. The shrapnel will strike hard and deep and wound all of us and yet Sabrina will walk away unscathed.

The next morning Sabrina subtly waited until I went to work and as soon as I left the house she went to my beautiful bride and said in her new baby voice, as tears rolled down her innocent cheeks, "Mom, I don't want to cause more of a problem than I've already caused, but last night when Dad took me to Albertson's he got really mad and backhanded me in my chest." Sabrina anxiously waited for her mother's response. What would Sarah's response be?

My wife Sarah had the biggest decision thus far on the roller coaster ride Sabrina had taken us on. Would she think with her head and realize that when Sabrina came home the night before that she was calm and unhurt in any way? Or would she think with her emotions and rescue her now distraught, lonely abused daughter?

Sarah was in a twixt between two and she regrettingly fed the monster within Sabrina and betrayed my trust. She aligned herself temporarily with her coercisive daughter and joined Sabrina's newly assembled team of rescuers. Sabrina hugged her mother and said, "I knew I could count on you, Mother, you're the best!" I can see Sabrina as she walks away from Sarah laughing under breath. She must have been thinking, people in this family are so gullible, ha-ha.

Sabrina has now intricately spread her web of deceit over the heart and eyes of my wife, my son and my daughter. I, too, have been used by Sabrina as a pawn for her against authority figures in the past. I understand the traps Sabrina laid for my wife and family and friends because, me, her very own father has gone on rescue missions for her against abusive people who disagreed with her.

Just one year ago she had an art teacher that she told me was ridiculing her, insulting her and verbally abusing her during class. I was pissed off at him before I even heard his story. Who would talk down to a national honor society student like my smart, competent daughter? Sabrina had loaded me up with her victim's mentality and unleashed me as an assault rifle at her art teacher.

When I talked to one of the vice-principals she informed that she's observed this class before and Sabrina talks back, and maligns this teacher in front of everybody. I did the same thing my innocent wife had done and had taken the bait from Sabrina and ran with it.

When Sabrina came home from school I confronted her concerning her behavior. She immediately said, "You're right, Dad, I'm sorry." She was willing to destroy this art teacher for no reason at all. What was she willing to do to our family?

Fasten your seatbelts and hold onto the rails because this roller coaster ride is just beginning! Hold on tight because there are so many more twists and turns my heart is racing just thinking about them!

CHAPTER 6

The Deposition

In this chapter you will see how Sabrina begins to put all of her information together and form alliances that will help her to win her case in the court of public opinion. Up until this point we have seen her enlist and recruit one co-dependant rescuer at a time. Now she will begin combining certain pre chosen "AL QUEDA" members and commissioning them to do her dirty work. (Together everyone accomplishes more)

She must have thought, I've given Ellen, Michael, Mom and certain friends just enough information to wet their appetite, but now I will light the flame of the atom bomb and no one will even remember all I did to ignite the flames of destruction in my formerly happy home.

It was a Saturday morning when I left to work my grueling fifteen hour day. I had no idea that this would be the final day my 15 year old daughter would ever stay at my home at 1118 Acemerry Ave. Shawnee, Oklahoma. "OPERATION DIVISION" was in full swing.

Sabrina had thrown out the "A" word of abuse and my naïve wife had clamped down on it like a shark and Sabrina was reeling Sarah into

31

her sinister plot.   My sweet, caring, thoughtful wife of two decades temporarily saw Sabrina (her baby girl) as "THE VICTIM" and not the culpable, defiant, manipulative teenager she had become.

In a moment of haste, Sarah took our daughters without my knowledge to Peter and Tosha Swaggert's home to inquire their advice concerning what to do in this perilous situation. I wish I could have stopped my distraught wife from going to the Swaggert's. They were dealing with a daughter themselves who while living at their house was unmarried with one child out of wedlock and another one on the way.

As the Swaggert's listened Sabrina began to explain, "Peter and Tosha, you both know I would never, ever do anything to cause anyone to think less of my Dad, but I really need to inform ya'll and others to the highest degree of accuracy that I've been wounded by my father and I'm scared." Sabrina started to cry as Peter, Tosha, Sarah, Ellen and the Swaggert's daughters all began hugging her and reaffirming her worth and value in spite of her father's angry, unjustifiable actions.

They all decided that the best plan of action would be to catch me off guard at another opportune time and sit me down in my own house and take my deposition. As they organized the time of questioning, it was agreed that this event would take place on Sunday when I got off work at approximately 9 p.m.

This was about to be the biggest surprise of my young 41 year old life. The planes were loaded with the enemy ammo and were headed to my humble abode to drop off one hell of a payload. It reminds me of the Japanese secretly flying under radar towards Pearl Harbor to bomb us unsuspecting Americans! Here I am, an American Dad about to be the recipient of Sabrina's counter attack! Oh, the waskily webs we weave.

Everyone was asleep when I came home from my 15 hour work day on Saturday night. Before I go to bed I always walk the hall and make sure all is well with my family before I hit the hay. I opened Sabrina's door to her bedroom and much to my dismay there was no Sabrina. Where was our sweet, innocent daughter? Was Clifford in the house? My mind began to do flashbacks from the previous two weeks.

I then opened Ellen's bedroom door and lo and behold Sabrina was snuggled up next to the safe, secure and loving arms of her older sister. I didn't have a clue at the time that for security reasons Sabrina was being protected by her older sister from her newly abusive father. Ellen was now on the secret service security team and part of her deployment was to help Sabrina in any and every way possible. (til death do us part!)

On Sunday morning I woke up to go to work and no one was in the house. I assumed that my wife and co–dependant daughters were gone to church to hear a good sermon on how to obey your parents in the Lord and honor your father and mother. Later that night I began calling Ellen and Sarah on their cell phones from my newly acquired cell phone that use to belong to Sabrina. The phones rang, but there was no answer, just silence, dead silence.

I walked through my front door and there was total quietness, no one was home. It was the proverbial calm before the storm. We were in the eye of the hurricane and the fury of Sabrina's deception was about to be unleashed upon the ultimate authority figure in her life, "THE FATHER". I went into my bedroom all alone and took a refreshing bath after a very busy work week.

The next words I heard would surprise me. It was Sarah's voice and she said, "Kevin the Swaggert's are here and they want to talk to you." Due to the previous two weeks of Sabrina's deeds coming to light and being exposed my first thoughts were that Sabrina was pregnant and the Swaggert's were there to help us get through this tumultuous time. They had been through so much as well meaning ministers and yet they were unable to keep their own daughters legs closed long enough to say,

"Our daughter's knocked up a second time out of wedlock under the liberal care of our home."

When I walked into my living room, Peter said, "Kevin, please have a seat." Looking back, I should have told Peter and Tosha to exit my abode and don't let the door hit you where the good Lord split you. Why were they in my home and why the hell are they asking me to sit down?

Let the usurping of my God given authority begin. Webster's defines usurping as: to exercise possession wrongfully, to supplant, to take the place of another by force. Peter and Tosha were armed with Sabrina's new weapon of abuse and were getting ready to fire a round right into my backside. Ouch, I wasn't expecting the knives to penetrate so deeply. Sabrina was outside in a car praying for me while I was completing my first deposition.

For some unknown reason I sat down and Peter opened with, "Kevin, we know what you've done to Sabrina. That sweet little daughter of yours has let us know your dirty little secret that you hit her." He also added that Sabrina told her that Michael confided in her that he too had been assaulted by his former children's pastor, namely, YOU!

I was on one couch while Peter, Tosha and my temporarily confused wife all had their arms crossed, sitting on the opposite couch, eagerly waiting for my reply as they peered at me with the dreaded 'EVIL EYE'. How would I respond ? Would I drop my pants and allow Sabrina through the avenue of loved ones to castrate me while I willingly accepted her punishment for challenging her rebellious behavior? Hell no! I pulled my pants up, pulled out the yarn stitched my balls back up and said, "She's a liar, and I'm calling the police, because there won't be a mark on her!!!!"

Peter and Tosha were escorted out and I snapped my wife back into reality and said, "We're calling the girls and they're coming home and we're going to stop this foolishness." We called the girls who were with one of Ellen's friends who had recently miscarried after getting knocked up by her boyfriend and said, "Get home, Sabrina's a liar!"

As the girls walked in the house I told Sabrina to go into one bedroom and Ellen into another room. Sarah and I started off by telling Ellen that she no longer had to co- dependently rescue her sister for lying, sneaking out and deceiving her family, friends and relatives. Ellen responded with a look that she enjoyed her enabling role and said, "I'm sooooo confused."

About this time Sabrina was slowly sneaking out of the bedroom and disobeying my instructions to stay in the other room. My little wild bronco was ready to let out an academy award performance. She came into Ellen's room and said, "DAD, you're not going to lie about all this, are you?" Can you imagine the shock I felt that first of all she wouldn't stay in the room I told her to, but that she would defiantly verbally attack me for my indiscretions? My behavior was now the issue----DECEPTION!

Before I could set Sabrina straight and explain why our family was being flushed down the toilet by her, she let out a blood curdling scream. She opened our front door and yelled, "Oh my God everybody, my Dad is not being truthful!" She was acting so good her body was convulsing and tears were rushing down her beautiful face as they did when she conveyed her rescuing story a few days earlier as Sarah and her cried together. Oh, the power of estrogen!

About this time Ellen grabs her cell phone and runs outside to tend to her baby sister's desperate needs. Ellen now had a new motto, it said, "United we stand, divided we fall." My daughters had formed an unbreakable bond, united by co-dependant rescuing and severe emotional manipulation. We truly were a house divided and no one even remembered any of the details of Sabrina's actions. She had succeeded in finding her scapegoat. In her mind I had kneeled before her and she laid her hands on my head and said, "You my Father, shall bear the guilt and the judgment that I should take." She was finally free, free at last!!!!

This is just the beginning of Sabrina's traveling ministry. She would now head to friends, family, schools and other cities carrying her message of victimization. Will she find more card carrying adults with a 'victim mentality' to rescue her, or will she finally get the help she so desperately needs? We shall see, we shall see!

CHAPTER 7

Bon Voyage – The Girls Are on the Run

The following day Sarah and I went to eat at one of our favorite restaurants in Shawnee called Bobby's Bar-b-q. While ordering we by chance happened to run into Justin Montana who works for the United States Post Office. His daughter is the girl who was driving the getaway car the night before when our girls made a run for it.

Justin is a good old country boy from Oklahoma who just seems like an even– keeled, hard working man. His wife on the other hand has had immense emotional problems, and had to deal with horrible tragedies in her life. She's very overweight, slurs her speech and really seems incapable of taking care of herself. My wife and I really respected Justin for being the backbone in his family in spite of having such a dysfunctional wife.

Our daughters had been there for Justin's daughter when she got pregnant and then miscarried. They definitely parent different than my wife and I. They were in the process of making plans for the boy who knocked their daughter up to move into their house and live with them until the horrible miscarriage. I can promise you that wouldn't have happened in my home!

As we conversed with Justin regarding the sad state of affairs that now existed in our once functional home he mentioned that he would temporarily house the girls until all this strife blew over. Sarah and I, having never had to deal with co-dependant teen-agers thought about it and accepted Justin's kind-hearted gesture. We figured one more night at a familiar place and the girls would be ready to come back home and sleep in their own beds and put all this high school drama stuff behind them.

I definitely believe Justin had good intentions at the beginning or I wouldn't have allowed the girls to stay with their family. At the time he seemed like an angel sent from heaven. Little did I know that when his wife got her dysfunctional hands on the situation that they would be like an angel of light sent from hell to steal, kill and destroy. The monster within Sabrina was about to learn firsthand from Liza how the grown up monster in her could take Sabrina's 'Operation Division' to an even higher level.

The first night the girls stayed at the Montana's house the monster within Liza began to pull out any and all pertinent information that could be used against me and defend sweet, innocent Sabrina. Can you hear Liza in her south Texas draw and Paula Abdul slurred speech saying, "Sabrina, I was wounded by my father years ago (she pulls up her shirt and shows her broken and contrite heart)and I'm here as a enabling, co-dependant rescuer to help you hate all men!"

Sabrina leans over and hugs Liza and as they both tear up Sabrina says, "Liza, when I was with my dad in the car that horrible, fateful night he got extremely angry at me." When Liza heard those words she called upon her anger and bitterness from her past experiences of emotional and physical traumas and told Sabrina, "You, my dear one are finally safe, Momma Liza will help you hold onto your hurt and pain and show you the right path to walk therein." (SCARY)

If you haven't figured it out yet, relationships are like a magnet. You are drawn to either healthy or unhealthy people without even cognizantly thinking about it. If you are dysfunctional then you will be drawn into the arms of people who emulate how you feel, think and believe life is and should be. Sabrina as a hormonally imbalanced teenager was being led, like a magnet to people just like herself. You will see in the coming chapters that anyone who believed in personal responsibility and owning up to your own actions are totally repulsive to Sabrina! (Beware; more bad counsel is on the way).

Liza was now rescuing her hurt, inner, unhealed child and going after my daughters to plant the seeds deeper inside of them that were already a blossomed tree of bitterness within her heart and bearing fruit of mistrust, anger and a deep sense of I'm THE VICTIM! She was about to get out her big pair of scissors that she hadn't used since her childhood and show Ellen and Sabrina how to place the scissors right near their father's ball sack and in the name of Oprah and Rosie with one unified squeeze yell, "MAKE HIM A GELDING, MAKE THEM ALL GELDINGS!" hahahahaha(snap)

Sabrina observes Liza's unbelievable boldness and gleans from the experienced veteran. Liza would show my girls how you have to know the way to show the way and then go the way. She would use great leadership skills to nurture her new team of rescuers and enablers. Liza does what any well meaning deceitful communicator would do and drives my daughter to child protective services to file a false report against the dreaded, evil 'FATHER FIGURE'. Sabrina must be thinking, this is a new level Liza's taking me to. I like it. Nobody will soon remember an inkling of what I did. Hahahaah. (You're on your own papa, it's us against you, BIG BOY.)

Sabrina, now being thoroughly empowered by Liza "THE MULE" Montana must be thinking, I, through this gift of manipulation can sway adults to do my will on earth as it is in my teenage emotions. The main two lessons Sabrina gleaned from Liza's wealth of knowledge in manipulating others was: 1. Men are evil and girls are sweet. 2. When in doubt always use the hurt woman card. Liza then whispers in Sabrina's ear as she lays her hand on her head and says, "Americans nowadays are stupid, they always go for the sad story." They both smile at each other and resume OPERATION DIVISION.

With Liza's help Sabrina was courageous enough to take every bit of the attention off her and dump it squarely on my big shoulders, an American Dad. In the emotional realm it is as if Liza, Ellen and Sabrina are all sneaking over to my house and simultaneously pushing out an incredibly huge dump on my front lawn and wow, does it stink!

Liza was probably happy to have all the attention off her formerly pregnant daughter and have another family with some problems to focus on. As I look back on all this I'm amazed at how the two families that hindered the healing process the most were families that had their own daughter's knocked up and couldn't stop it. Liza was now calling the school district and any and all other families who would join the enabling and rescuing team, can you say Al Anon!

One day Liza mustered up enough xanax courage to actually call me. Here's what she said in her mumbling southern voice, "Kevin, when I was little my daddy was mean to me." Also, she in unintelligible speech conveyed that her and her husband in a heated moment with their teenage daughter held her down and beat her with a belt. I stopped her and said, "Why are you telling me your testimony of dysfunction?" She then said something I'll never forget, "I want to be your daughter's new Mama!"

40

We had to get our daughters out of this horrendous situation. But how? They were hunkered down almost to the point of having ankle monitors on our daughter's feet. Sarah and I began devising a plan that I now call 'OPERATION RESCUE'. In the next chapter you will see how tightly the web of deception was wound around our daughters' souls.

CHAPTER 8

Operation Rescue

I know some of you out there are wondering why my wife and I didn't take the bull by the horns and just go and retrieve our two formerly obedient daughters. That's a legitimate question and one that I completely concur. Have you ever looked back on a situation and thought of ways you could have and should have done something a little different? Hindsight in this situation is 20-20.

We, in our defense had never had even an inkling of a major problem in our home. Maybe that's why we all handled everything so poorly. We should have let our kids overcome a few speed bumps in the road instead of protecting their sweet, innocent souls. Our desire as parents was that we wanted our kids to have a great childhood and probably looking back we were too easy on them. I wish I could go back and be a better disciplinarian and remove some of that bound-up selfishness and foolishness. We erred on the side of caution.

No matter how we got to this point in our relationship with our unhealthy co-dependant daughters, that's where we are and we must look ahead and try to rectify the situation. My wife and I had to devise a plan to get our daughters out of the lioness clutches of the Montana compound. How could we rip our kids out of their control? They had latched down on our daughters like a lion clamps down on its prey and were hunkered down and not willing to give up their two newly, emotionally kidnapped daughters.

The Montana's had usurped our authority as Sabrina's and Ellen's parents and further fed the monster within Sabrina that justified her behavior and villainized me, an American Dad. Instead of upholding the authority of the parent, they had agreed with two drama filled teenagers. No wonder their daughter was knocked up in their own house, under their direct supervision.

The stakes were high, but the expedition had to be executed to deliver our confused manipulating daughters. But where would we send Sabrina? She was out of control and not willing to be tamed in any way, shape or form. She was like a lion going to and fro seeking someone to devour! We had to cage her, even if it meant Ellen and she would have to be separated from each other emotionally. How could they survive without each other? They would rather die than be separated from their emotional Siamese connection.

We called and talked to our good friends Ben and Abigail Arnold who highly suggested a Christian girl's home in Norman, Oklahoma about 20 miles from our home. Sarah and I talked and we decided to contact the Shelter of Love and see if, by chance they could quickly take in our little bucking bronco. When we met with the directors they had heard we were good parents with temporarily deranged daughters and willingly accepted to take our LITTLE HITLER into their semi-locked down facility.

Finally we believed we were headed in the right direction with our main goal to get Sabrina the psychological help she so desperately needed. But how would we rescue Sabrina from the clutches of Madame Liza? She was emotionally breastfeeding the girls, one on each pap on the sincere milk of fear, rejection and hatred for all authority figures.

This would have to be a covert operation due to the land mines placed all around the Montana's home. How could we get Sabrina to get in the car without one hell of a scene? Our plan was for Sarah to call Sabrina and say she wanted to take her to get a drink and to talk some stuff over. Maybe Sabrina thought her mother could be re-enlisted and could be swayed by some good crying or yelling?

Sarah put on her camouflage, painted her eyes, strapped her guns on and went after her daughter like an under cover swat team on a night mission. She made the call and sure enough Sabrina took the bait and was preparing herself as Sarah was driving to the Montana's compound. Hurry, honey before Liza discerns through her divination that you're trying to rip her new girl's from her breasts.

Sarah drives up to the home and Sabrina comes and sits in the car. I wish Sarah could have driven off right then and there before Ellen gets into the car and emboldens Sabrina to further rebel against her formerly good parents. But sure enough Liza discerned something was wrong while she was at work and called her daughter and asked how the wounded girls were doing? That's when Liza's daughter received the instruction to not let Sabrina get in the car without Ellen being there to protect her.

Liza's daughter yells to Ellen, "My mom says it's not safe for Sabrina to be with her mother. Hurry Ellen don't let her go!!!" Ellen runs out of the house like a track star, barely clothed and dives into the backseat, just in time. She must have been thinking, good, my sweet, adorable sister is not alone and never will be. I will never leave her or forsake her. (Together forever, til death do us part)

While Sarah was driving the getaway car to the semi –locked down facility I was at a good friend's son's football game. I informed him of operation rescue and we both had a bad feeling about Ellen emboldening Sabrina to not obey or submit to her newly dysfunctional parents. When Sarah arrived at the Shelter of Love the directors were waiting for Sabrina's arrival. They should have had a straight jacket prepared along with a tazer gun to control our little raging teenager.

Once Sabrina knew that this would be her new home she stood up and began releasing the most profanity-laced tyrade imaginable. She looked at Ellen for support and they both said to one another, "We're getting the hell out of here!" Sabrina went for the phone to call the Montana's to come rescue them, but the director said to Sabrina, "Put the phone down!" Sabrina temporarily obeyed his command before Ellen and she made a run for it into the cold dark night. As they were running down the lonely road Sarah jumped into the car and found them and said, "Get in the car, now!" They got into the car, it filled the car with strife, division and total confusion.

Sarah then called me and was justifiably embarrassed and distraught. She told me what just transpired and I was very sorry I missed such a fun, adventurous night. There would be plenty more adventurous nights I would be a part of in the future.

Our initial plan of placing Sabrina at this semi-locked down facility didn't work, but at least they were out of the Montana compound. One victory at a time, inch by inch it's a cinch, yard by yard it's hard.

Where do we go from here? Can someone throw us a lifeline? I think my wife and I are drowning and Ellen and Sabrina are holding our heads under the water. Help, I can't breathe, can you honey? Sabrina replies, "Good, that's the way I planned it all!"

CHAPTER 9

Flashback to Sabrina's Childhood

Sabrina was born on June 21,1989 at Thompkins Hospital in Tulsa, Oklahoma. Sarah decided to have Sabrina completely natural. I wasn't so sure that was a good idea; a digital block seemed to be a lot less painful. But Sarah is a real trooper and I stood by her decision 100%.

When it came time for Sabrina to come into our lives and her little head began crowning (that's coming out of the womb to the layman), my wife began to let out a harmonious scream. The uncompassionate doctor who was experiencing no pain at all told my wife, "Hey, pipe down, it's not that painful!" I don't know if he's ever had his legs blared in stirrups with an 8 lb. object protruding from his lower extremities, but it sure as hell looked like it hurt to me! The only thing I told my wife I could compare childbirth to was being real constipated. She said, "Not even close, not even close!"(Ouch)

When Sabrina was born Sarah and I lifted her up and dedicated her to the Lord and said, "Lord, we give this beautiful girl into your hands. Please give her a great life and help us to be a big blessing to her." Sabrina would be our final baby and hopefully we had learned from the previous two how to be better parents and impact her in a positive way.

The first four years of Sabrina's life we lived at 534 Sequilla Drive in Oklahoma City, Oklahoma in a beautiful 3 bedroom, 2 bath home. It was in a perfect location for having three small children. It was located on a cul-de-sac where the kids could play outside without fearing the oncoming traffic. The house also had a built in patio that the kids made into their own personal playhouse. We had awesome neighbors that had children approximately our kid's ages and they all played very well together.

I worked Monday through Friday so the weekends were especially fun for me. We enrolled the kids in sports throughout the calendar year and loved going on family outings to watch them compete in different sporting events. I may be a little partial, but all 3 of my kids were superior athletes and good looking at that!

On Saturday night Sarah and I prepared for Sunday mornings by cooking lunch for the next day and getting the car packed for the next morning's jaunt to church. Why would we get ready on Saturday night? The church we went to for the first 4 years of Sabrina's life was 2 hours away in Catulla, Oklahoma. I look back now and can't believe we traveled that far every week for over 200 weeks in a row. The fact is that we loved the country, the pastor and the people and we also had some relatives who attended the same church. Oh the virility of youth.

Sarah and I would wake the kids up and leave the house by 7 am and arrive at the church by 9 am and unload the car and start volunteering our time to serve others. The trip was so comfortable in our spacious 2-door Toyota Corolla with 3 small children sprawled out all over the car. We've got great memories of all the precious time we spent together. Thanks, Sarah for all your time and effort you put into being the best mom in the whole world! She loves not in word or tongue but in deed and truth.

Once we arrived at church Sarah and I began working and the kids started playing and having a fun time. I served as a greeter, usher and Sunday school teacher, while Sarah was in charge of the entire children's church services. We made an awesome one – two punch! I hope you're getting the picture that my wife and I are the most incredible, talented parents of all time! I humbly concur! Thank you, thank you very much.

After the services we either took the kids out to eat at the one restaurant in town or went to friend's house and ate with them and took one heck of a nap. The Oklahoma Hill country has the most beautiful scenic views in the world. It's loaded with rivers and streams and tall trees and mountains that make it a natural paradise. What a place to raise the best kids in the whole world. I better move on to the facts, I'm getting a little choked up thinking of how good it use to be.(I do miss those days with my family.)

After Sunday night church we'd load up the car and head back to Oklahoma City. Sarah would drive home and I'd sleep with the kids since I had to be at work the next morning at 5am. When we arrived at the house the kids would rush off to sleep while Sarah and I would unload the car and get ready for the upcoming week. (Memories of the way we were).

I'm in a deep moment of reflecting upon Sabrina's child hood and for the life of me cannot remember anything that would be remotely responsible for her now dependant, manipulative behavior? Why the sudden change? Where did the deep anger come from? Are her actions mine and my wife's fault? Or is she ultimately responsible for her own behavior? Maybe we do need a licensed professional cuckoo to help us get out of the fog she created?

The only memory from Sabrina's childhood and formative years that I can think of that had any impact on her innocent soul was when we purchased our first dog. We rescued a dog that was part chow and part lab from the SPCA. We named her Goldie. She was a young teething dog that really loved to bite and claw. The first night we brought her home we put her in the backyard and played with her for a bit and then went inside to have dinner. I went outside to check on her and she was gone. She'd climbed under the fence and was across the street at the neighbor's house watching the neighbor work on his car. Goldie had forsaken us after we had rescued her from certain death. She had betrayed us and left us for a neighbor. Let's don't get to melodramatic, she's only a dog!

Goldie wouldn't stop biting and clawing the kids so we had to get rid of her and return her to the SPCA. The next morning after I went to work Sarah called the SPCA and they said they would come pick Goldie up around noon. When they arrived at our house Sarah told the kids to go to their rooms and said, "Don't look out the window." What do you think our kids did? Michael and Ellen ran into our bedroom and saw Goldie collared, chained and drug away never to be seen again. The funny thing is that Sabrina ran to the wrong window and looked out the back of the house and was spared the heartache that Michael and Ellen would now have to through. Honest to goodness that's the only memory our kids ever faced in their formative years that possibly could have had any negative connotations.

Are we getting soft in America? Or is it just my family? Could we be so concerned with our children's fragile emotions that they're not learning any coping skills? Could this bomb that Sabrina lit in our home be an indicator that we Americans are turning into little wimps? Are all of our counseling and prescription drugs really helping us be a stronger nation? Why don't we ask Anna Nicole and her son and see if all the drugs and counseling made them stronger and less co-dependant people?

If Sabrina had a million dollar childhood consisting of love, security and a wealth of friendships and support then why the extreme change? Why the deception? Where did all the dysfunction come from? Did she expect others to move at her every whim and wham, and did she really value the child hood she was blessed with? I think whether you're raised by functional or dysfunctional parents you and I have a choice and free will to perceive every situation with either eyes of truth and mercy or with the jaded glasses of selfishness. How did they treat me? The question should be how did you respond? That's when freedom comes, when you and I take responsibility for our personal actions and reactions. I think it's time we put Dr. Phil and Oprah and all the great wise counselors out of business and quit patty-caking each other and say, "Rise up, forgive and be a conqueror and not the victim!"

IT"S NOT AS IMPORTANT WHAT HAPPENS TO YOU AS WHAT HAPPENS IN YOU!!!!!! (SELAH)

CHAPTER 10

A Temporary Safe House

Sarah calls me on the phone hysterically and frantically saying, "Kevin, please help me, the girls are out of control. This is the worst day of my life!" I envisioned the girls driving a locomotive train right through the middle of our home. Sabrina was the captain and Ellen was the assistant putting the coals in the oven of the train. As they're going down the track at 100 mph they see the Montana family on the side of the road smiling and waving as proud co-dependant enablers. The Montanas hold up a thumbs up sign and yell, "That's our girls, we're so proud of your rebellion, roll right over your parents and shame them in front of everybody!" (choo, choo)

Despite the meddling, dysfunctional and co-dependant Montana family we have the very best friends a person could have. It's taken us over 12 years to build some beautiful healthy relationships and in spite of Sabrina's attempt to huff and puff and blow our house down, we would and will stand! One such family is the Barber family. Our daughters have played soccer and gone to school with them for almost 10 years. Samantha has served the community as an educator for over two decades and her husband John is a loan officer with a great head on his shoulders.

I called Samantha and informed her concerning our daughters' crazy attempt to steal, kill and destroy from our family's sanity and peace of mind. She responded by saying, "Kevin, I'm aware of the situation and know and believe ya'll can work through this." It was encouraging to have some well meaning, non-codependent friends to intervene. Samantha and John temporarily said they'd house our gypsy girls under these conditions: 1. That we went to a counselor. 2. Everyday worked toward reconciliation. But could and would Sabrina loosen her strangle hold on our family and humble herself to participate or would she roar like a lion until there was only bits and pieces of our once happy family left. We shall see. We shall see.

Samantha has influenced hundreds of families in a positive way and one such person was a pastor's family who had some real problems with their son. She talked to this pastor and he agreed to meet with our family for $50.00 a visit. He met with the girls first and then with us parents. After the initial meeting which totaled $100.00 he decided to have my precious wife meet alone with the angry, abandoned Sabrina.

Sarah walks into the room as the pastor and Sabrina are waiting for her to come in. Sabrina had received these instructions before Sarah came into the office by the LPC pastor. "Sabrina, I want you to write on a piece of paper all the things you hate about your mother and if it gets tough while you're reading it, I'll help you through it." Sabrina hugs the pastor as they pray together. The pastor then tells our once submissive daughter this story, "Sabrina, my dad was an alcoholic and he's dead now and I've never gotten over the shameful, abusive way he treated me." We had been set up again! This pastor was a licensed professional cuckoo. I wish I could have told Sarah to get the hell out of that office before Sabrina and this pastor both regurgitate on her.

Sarah sits down and has no idea the devastation just around the corner. Sabrina pulls out the paper and with the pastors help begins to read, "I hate you Mom for this, this, this and this." My sweet wife who bore our daughter 15 years before had no idea that the monster within Sabrina would wreck such havoc in her soul. Why? We don't understand, Sabrina, why? Before Sarah leaves the room and pays $50.00 she has to reach down and pick up her heart that her daughter just sliced out of her chest!

Why would this pastor validate such rebellion in our daughter who was straying away so fast? Did we run into another co-dependant rescuer who hates his own father? Is he carrying a big pair of scissors like Rosie and Oprah? Did his father come in and play late night sneaky, sneaky? Beware church, the monster has snuck in behind the pulpit and he's roaring and slicing all in its pathway! This pastor must have ripped out the pages in his Bible that say, "Honor your mother and father."

Sarah called me crying and said, "Kevin, you won't believe what just happened. Sabrina ripped me to shreds and I'm hurting, please help me." When Sarah conveyed to me the perilous situation that she just faced I tried to comfort her and then hung up the phone and drove up to the parsonage to confront the evil pastor.

I walked into the office and sat this pastor down and asked him what the hell was going on? He then told me the story of his deep hatred towards his father and how he could never allow an authority figure to squash an innocent child again. This was the last meeting and $50.00 I'd ever pay this so-called pastor to put a bigger wedge in our family than was already there.

How could Sabrina ever see clearly through all the fog of adults who co-dependently rescued her and defended her and villainized her once caring and thoughtful parents? I immediately called the Barber's and they agreed that this pastor was giving some bad advice to our family. It was an innocent mistake, who would have thought a pastor would be filled with such anger towards authority figures?

In the meantime Sabrina was tightening the noose around her older sister's neck to rescue her. Late at night Sabrina rolled over in bed and woke Ellen up and said, "Ellen, I'm going to kill myself for all the things I've done to our family." Ellen jumped up and started crying and said, "You will not do that and I will never leave you and never forsake you." Sabrina hugged Ellen and smiled as she realized the noose still fit perfectly around her older sister's neck. As a co-dependant Sabrina was thrilled to see that she wasn't alone! She then told Ellen, "You're my best friend in the whole world!"

The next morning as the girls were getting up preparing themselves for school Mr. Barber noticed that as always Sabrina was the last one to get up and never helped in any way around the house. She was always staying up late and watching MTV and leaving the lights on all night long and playing on the computer until 3 or 4 a.m. Mr . Barber was growing wearing of the selfish dependant attitude Sabrina was exhibiting. He's a person who believes in personal responsibility and that was not sitting well with Sabrina as she had a need to be rescued 24/7. (She's the baby girl)

Mr. Barber and I discussed a plan to get together and sort through some junk and try to communicate before Sabrina ended up in foster care. The next day we arrived at the Barber home and sure enough everyone began talking and catching up on what was happening in our now separate lives, except for one individual. You guessed it, everybody except Sabrina, 'THE VICTIM'. Mr. Barber confronted Sabrina and said, "Hey, Sabrina, did you know that your mom and dad were here?" It was evident right then and there that there would be no reconciliation while the girls were at the Barber's house due to Sabrina not being through with her sinister plan to tie me and her mother to the end of a vehicle and drag us through the town bloodied and beaten!

Before we could admit Sabrina into Teen Connection, Ellen was getting homesick and told Sabrina, "I'm ready to go home, enough is enough." What would Sabrina do? I knew she had to have the allegiance of another person to feel secure. She then said, "I'm ready to go home also." Why the sudden change, I thought Sabrina was so strong she could stand alone! It was time to split the emotional Siamese twins up once and for all!

I will always be grateful to the Barber's for their true friendship and desire to help us tame the beast within Sabrina. My daughter's have never spoken to the Barber's from that day to this. Why? Because they're a healthy, functional family that believes like I do in personal responsibility. This is mean and selfish to co-dependant people like my daughters'. ('til death do us part)

Ellen's coming home and Sabrina's going to be all alone amongst other girls who have some serious problems. Sabrina would be temporarily caged like a wild animal. Will she finally come to her senses or will there be other co-dependant people that rescue their own hurt inner child by rescuing our little baby girl? We shall see.

CHAPTER 11

A Semi-Locked Down Facility

When we took Sabrina to the local TEEN CONNECTION facility she became very docile and withdrawn. Her soul looked empty and defeated as her plans in operation division were temporarily thwarted. The monster within my little darling had been caged and separated from her main co-dependant team member, Ellen 'the enabler'. How would Ellen and Sabrina survive without the dysfunctional support of each other? Would they have to each begin to take personal responsibility for their own actions?

The first week Ellen and Sabrina were abruptly divided without their permission Ellen would come home in tears, uncontrollably sobbing for her long lost sister. My thoughtful wife would take our oldest daughter shopping or to the grocery store and all Ellen could say to her mother was, "Mom, do you ever miss Sabrina?" as huge cow tears streamed like a flowing river down Ellen's once happy face. Sarah tried to encourage Ellen that it was okay for her to be happy and free even if her sister was temporarily in someone else's care. Isn't it prideful for Ellen to think she is a better parent than her mother and me? The scales of deception over Ellen's eyes regarding her sister were adhered with super glue!

One of the counselors at Teen Connection arranged a meeting between me, Sarah and our little bucking bronco. Before Sarah and I left for another gut wrenching episode in "Teenage Drama 101" I told my wife, "I'm not holding back anything with Sabrina, she's going to hear exactly what she hates, the TRUTH." I was prepared to rip Sabrina a new one and remind her that we were and are the thoughtful loving parents we've always been and that we hadn't changed but she changed right about the time she started her menstural cycle 4 months before the blow up. I knew co-dependants hate the truth and that they perceive people who speak the truth without any sugarcoating as mean, non- caring and insensitive people.

As my wife and I walked into the room and closed the door behind us I beheld my youngest daughter looking in total disarray. Her face was broken out in pimples, her hair was a mess and she looked helpless and all alone. Instead of lashing out at her for all the troubles and heartache she had drug our family through I was hit in the face with the fact that I totally love this girl and want the best for her life.

My emotions took over and I began to literally weep as I told Sabrina, "I love you so much and I'm sorry for everything that's led us to this point, please forgive me and let's start over." There wasn't a dry eye in the room as Sarah, the counselor and Sabrina had all joined me in the parade of tears. Would this be the end of the anger, the divisiveness and the total turmoil in our once happy American home?

This meeting was a good start, but my wife and I knew that Sabrina needed some help as to why she villianized and deceived so many people to rescue her. We wanted her to stay and get some help from some good counseling. Sabrina thought that she should come home and be with Ellen and not be left all alone in a semi-locked down facility.

We all actually saw her countenance change right before us when she knew she wasn't coming home. She closed up like a turtle and went into a shell with the intent to emotionally punish her mother and me. Sabrina's defense mechanism was kicking in gear as she decided that she would be in control and not us. But how? How could she regain control? Who could she recruit to rescue and enable her? I hoped these counselors could help Sabrina with understanding her bi-polar, controlling behavior.

In Sabrina's mind she had erased the bountiful amount of love and forgiveness displayed by her mother and me as she began plotting once again on how to retaliate against the authority figure in her life with the victim card. I feel sorry for my once stable daughter as I reflect on what a blessing she used to be before she was caught in her web of lies? She would begin to reassemble a new team within the locked down facility that would help her, the baby daughter!

What was Sabrina's main tool and why were so many well meaning people falling prey to her skillful manipulation? Webster's defines manipulation as: to control or play upon by artful, unfair, or insidious means for ones own advantage. It also says manipulation is the process of changing by unfair means to serve ones own purpose. Sabrina was trying to change every person's view of what had transpired in our family in the last two months and I would have none of it, therefore I was the target of her attacks.

I could lie to myself and say that we're all to blame for these tragic events, but that would be a lie and full of false humility. It's not our fault and I'm sure there are some parents out there who blame themselves because you have had or have a little bucking bronco like me. Quit it! Don't allow yourself to say, "It's my fault because I got a divorce or I made this mistake or that mistake, no no no." That guilt is allowing the one you love to manipulate you. You are responsible for you and

I'm responsible for me. It's that simple. Let it go! Do you need your children's approval rating that bad?

Sabrina had hardened her heart as the Egyptians hardened their heart against the children of Israel. She didn't like the idea of her parents being free while she was in the bondage of a locked down facility like a caged animal. She would have to use her valuable manipulative resources to try to do further damage to her culpable parents. How could she deploy more bombs of destruction? She would not go down without one hell of a fight! Watch out Sarah, Sabrina wants to tie us to the back of a truck and drag us nude through our town to shame and bring further embarrassment to our once happy home!

Sabrina would begin assembling one lean mean fighting machine that could carry out her mission to steal, kill and destroy the very fabric of our family. Her first recruit would be a young, immature girl counselor. I can't even imagine what this lady's father did to her in the early morning hours that caused her such horrific pain? In her mind all men were evil, just like her damn father! This new counselor had a big pair of Rosie and Oprah scissors ready to emasculate another American father.

It was 2:00 p.m. on a Thursday afternoon that we went to the locked down facility to pick Sabrina and take her to her dentist appointment. From the time Sabrina got in the car until we arrived at the dentist office Sabrina looked possessed by the monster of bitterness. There were no words she said to her mother or me just grunts and groans. The monster had come back seven times worse than before.

On the way back from the dentist Sabrina asked if she could go see her older sister play in her state championship volleyball game that night. I replied, "Sabrina, I think it would be better at this time if you didn't and just kept working with your counselors on some serious issues." Are you ready for my sweet submissive daughters reply? She said, "Good, I don't want to go anyway and by the way ya'll are the worst parents in this whole f....... world!!" I turned around and faced the monster eyeball to eyeball and said, "You better watch your tone with me or there will be consequences!" Her eyes looked right through me as I observed the monster s piercing look of hatred.

We were three blocks from the locked down facility when Sabrina's anger changed into the baby voice as she began to cry and said, "You hate me, you hate me, why do you treat me this way, neither one of you love me, I'm all alone." As soon as we stopped the car Sabrina jumped out like a mad woman and as she ran into the facility she turned her head around on a swivel like Sybil and raised her middle finger and said, "F.... you!"

Needless to say things were not going as we had hoped at teen connection due to the fact Sabrina, the bucking bronco didn't want them to go well. If you haven't noticed, it takes two willing parties to reconcile and Sabrina and the monster within her were not going to comply until she was through emotionally whipping me and her mother with her big horse whip. (BAM, BAM)

This is when we went to plan "D", that's right plan "D". Plans A, B,and C were all unsuccessful at corralling the wild horse named Jezebel, I mean Sabrina. We, out of desperation and not wanting our daughter in foster care leaned on the advice of our friend and asked the Shelter of Love, which is a Christian girl's home to house our unstable daughter. They said they would and we made the necessary arrangements to remove Sabrina from teen connection and transport her to her new home.

The next day we went to teen connection and signed some paperwork and loaded up all of Sabrina's lifelong possessions into our Nissan Sentra and waited for her co-dependant, dad-hating counselor to bring out our little prisoner.   As Sabrina walks out of the facility she hugs the counselor as the counselor looks at me and her mother and says, "Are you sure this is what is best for this sweet little angel?" Sabrina, being empowered by Ellen's enabling replacement throws her backpack against the side window of the car as it almost breaks out the window.

Could this Christian girl's home help our daughter see the light, or was she headed down another twisted path of destruction? Is Sabrina going to be wise enough to dupe the directors into rescuing her or will they say a hearty no to usurping our authority and demand that Sabrina begin showing a little RESPECT. Read on and see the amazing outcome.

CHAPTER 12

On the Road Again

As we drove Sabrina out to the Shelter of Love in Norman , Oklahoma approximately 20 miles from our house we noticed that she was staring with a blank stare out the window into the heavenlies. We were severing all her previously made alliances of co-dependant relationships and she had no idea what the future held for her. Where were her formerly loving, caring and thoughtful parents dragging her to?

On the way out to the compound we stopped at a convenience store to get a drink and to give the director time to move Sabrina's new room from the bottom floor to the top floor in case she were to make another run for it. The director is older and slower than Sarah and I so there's no way he could have caught her with her superior athletic talent.

While I was in the convenient store purchasing the drinks Sabrina leaned up to the front seat and in a deep, sinister voice said to her mother figure, "Mom, you know this won't work, don't you?" She then actually let out a small hissing noise of sarcasm.

When we all arrived at the Shelter of Love the director met us and helped us as we brought all of Sabrina's belongings and put them in her new bedroom. Sabrina didn't help us; she just aimlessly walked around the compound surveying the new predicament she found herself in.

My wife and I said our goodbyes and as we left my thoughtful wife couldn't leave without hugging Sabrina and saying one more time, "I love you, Sabrina. I do love you!" My beautiful wife who bore our now rebellious daughter almost 16 years previously felt compelled to express to Sabrina how much she loved her in spite of Sabrina's deception, betrayal and heavy blows she belted our family with.

On the drive home my wife and I prayed for Sabrina to get the help she so desperately needed as we both continually cried and wondered how we had gotten as a family to the point we were currently in. Oh how the mighty had fallen!

Ellen the enabler had no idea that when she came home from school that day that her sister would be ripped from her life as a baby bird is ripped from the bosom of its mother. How could Ellen survive without having her baby sister to rescue and enable? Ellen more importantly thought how can Sabrina survive without me, her protector? I've got a news flash Ellen, you did a piss poor job in your role as a mother hen, just look at Sabrina and see the fruits of your labor?

We let a counselor tell Ellen of the horrific news of Sabrina's departure to a distant land and as we expected Ellen could barely walk when she heard the news. Her life flashed before her as she realized her and Sabrina were all alone. As Ellen walked in the house weeping and gnashing her teeth she questioned the sanity of her parent's decision that we made without her consent. She kept saying to us, "Why, why Mom and Dad, don't you love Sabrina as much as I do?" She asked how we could be so cold hearted to abandon her beautiful sister. Are you getting the point that Ellen had a completely warped view of true love?

One of the rules the Shelter of Love had for new arrivals was for there to be no, zero contact with parents and children for the first four months to help the recovery process. Although that seemed like a long time we were willing to comply with the edict for the good of our lost daughter's soul.

That is why when I went to the mailbox a week later I was completely shocked that in the mail was a letter from Sabrina with her mother's and my name x'd out and the letter was addressed to Ellen. I opened it up and sure enough Sabrina hadn't given up on re-recruiting Ellen back to her team. The letter was full of emotional manipulation as Sabrina talked about that someday, in this life or the next that they would be together forever. Wow!

I called the director and he apologized to me and said he'd have to do a better job of monitoring Sabrina. Was Sabrina using her slyness and prowess on this older man to seduce him to allowing her to get her way?

Sabrina went into the rehabilitation center in November and we hadn't talked to her since then. Christmas was one and a half months, except for the letter, that we had no contact with Sabrina. During Christmas the director went against his request for us to have no contact again and allowed Sabrina to call us on the telephone. Why would he again allow Sabrina to call? I was getting confused as to why the director asked us to do something he wasn't doing. Sabrina left the most gut wrenching call and deeply apologized for all the pain and sorrow she had caused our home.

I called and confronted the director about allowing my daughter to call and break the previously required rules. I said, "Hey Lester, I thought you wanted us to adhere to the request of no contact for four months." He replied, "Kevin, normally that is what we do, but Sabrina was so overwhelmed emotionally that we decided to allow her to break the rules this one time." This seemed a little odd to me, but maybe he knows better even though he and his wife have never had kids of their own.

After Sabrina left there was no more strife in our home town except for one more bizarre incident involving two of Sabrina's friends and a dad. The girl that Sabrina said she was going to her house when she was really on a secret rendezvous with her lover convinced her dad to drive her and a friend to my house to question me regarding the disappearance of Sabrina.

This nincompoop of a dad actually drove his car to my house and let his emotionally deranged daughter out of the car with her friend to question me. The dad wisely stayed in the car and didn't come to the door. That probably saved him a trip to the dentist, if you know what I mean.

When I opened the door I was surprised to see Hillary and Carol dripping in tears while they asked me, "Mr. Bassoon what is wrong with you and what prison did you put Sabrina in?" My reply was, "Girls I love you both, but it's none of your business, but if your dad wants to come talk to me mano y mano tell him to have at it." Hillary said, "Not going to happen." They left and I've never seen the drama queens again. It's amazing how my daughter was attracted to kids that were filled with drama. (Drama Mamas)

Please forgive me for a moment as I reflect on the people who offered their unsolicited advice regarding our lost daughter. There seems to be a pattern of those families that either usurped our authority or involved themselves in destructive ways in our moment of family crisis.

Let's ponder the pastor who told my daughter to lash out at her mother. What was his motive for being the almighty licensed professional cuckoo? He hated his dead alcoholic father for abusing him as a kid. How about the Montana's who temporarily kidnapped the girls? The mother actually helped hold down and beat their daughter. How about this last family that drove their kid to question me as she cried bigger tears than my manipulative daughter could have. They had unbelievable problems with their oldest daughter who they deemed the black sheep of the family.

Are you amazed at the people that are so willing to give advice when their homes are in total disarray? It reminds me of so many fat people who can tell you exactly what to eat to lose weight or the alcoholics who try to teach others about moderation being the key to success. If it ain't working in your house please don't come to my house and spread your so called wisdom!

I had to meddle a little bit to justify myself from all the busybodies that haven't looked in the mirror lately and realized that they've got enough to work on in their house before they rescue my now dysfunctional family.

For the next three months we had no contact with Sabrina and it is refreshing not having to deal with all the strife and discord. Is Sabrina finally turning a corner and being lassoed back to reality? Can this Christian girl's home help my lost daughter? Let's continue reading and we shall see together.

CHAPTER 13

True Repentance?

We, as a family had not had an inkling of strife and discord since Sabrina was taken to her new semi-locked down facility. The good book says, cast out the scoffer and strife will cease, yes, even dishonor. We were experiencing a sigh of relief, a temporary reprieve from all the teenage manipulative drama. Although we loved Sabrina, our emotions were getting a much needed time of refreshing.

When the month of March arrived we knew the 4 months were up and that Sabrina would soon be calling. Would the monster within her be tamed? Or would we be headed for another round of UFC style cage brawling? Our thoughts and prayers were that Sabrina would just go back to being the extreme blessing she was the first 15 years of her life.

The phone rings and I go over to see whose calling. We have a new thing called caller ID and you can see who's calling before you answer the phone. The number indicates its The Shelter of Love and sure enough it's Sabrina, our long lost daughter. I answered the phone and said, "Hello". Sabrina says, "Dad, it's me, your daughter." It's the first time in 7 months Sabrina has called me Dad. (She had been referring to me as Kevin). Her voice sounds so sincere.

She starts off with some small talk and then gets right to the point. She begins to cry and says, "Daddy, will you forgive me for lying about you and misrepresenting what really happened?" She said our family was the best home a girl could have been raised in. I replied, "Of course I do sweetheart, I love you and always have!" I then told my reborn daughter that we would treat all this as a speed bump in the road and that we would forget the past and reach forward to new beginnings in all of our lives. She was ecstatic and then she said something funny about what she missed the most the last several months. She said, "Dad, I never thought I'd miss all your farting and burping, but I have." I let her know that there were plenty more farts and burps left for her to enjoy! (Sorry for being gross)

After we hung up the phone I realized that Sabrina called me Dad throughout the entire phone conversation. I was no longer the evil authority figure, I was once again Dad. We had overcome and conquered our past mistakes and were headed in the right direction. The sun was shining in our hearts again and there was new hope for a better tomorrow in each of our lives.

Sabrina was now attending a Christian school, living in a protective environment and going to church two times a week. Her grades and conduct were returning to the way they were the first 15 years of her life. This must have been especially hard on Ellen. Here Sabrina is beginning to make big strides of improvement, honoring her father and mother, making good grades, etc, primarily because Ellen's enabling and co-dependant behavior was cut off from her life. Ellen must have thought to herself, I never was qualified to be her mother, I was just her sister. It's ok Ellen, you too were taken captive by the snare of the fowler of deception and led down a twisting and turning path of co-dependant rescuing.

We began talking with Sabrina on a consistent basis and were pleased with the progress she was making at the Shelter of Love. Inch by inch it's a cinch, yard by yard it's hard. She was doing well in a structured environment. Our home was way more relaxed and we allowed our kids to make a lot of decisions on their own. That worked for Michael and Ellen, but not for Sabrina, she needed more direction, more structure.

The director of the girl's home suggested that Sabrina begin coming home on the weekends and readjusting herself back into society. Lester would give Sabrina weekend passes and she would start coming home in April and begin integrating herself back into the family structure. We were not quite the happy, trusting family we once were, but we certainly weren't the capital "D" dysfunctional we had become before Sabrina left for the semi locked down facility.

I still remember talking with Ellen and Sarah about making Sabrina's homecoming a huge celebration. We all went to the store and bought balloons, streamers, and a big sign we put in the front yard that said, "WELCOME HOME!"

Sarah and I drove out to the Shelter of Love to get Sabrina and bring her home for the first time since she left in August. It had been seven months and I was excited and anxious to see her. I missed her smile, her laugh and so many other great things about her. She's coming home and I had all kinds of good emotions rushing through me.

We knocked on the door and the director opened the door and let us in. All of Sabrina's friends were waiting in the living room when we got there and they all gave us a big hearty welcome. Sabrina was upstairs when we arrived and we couldn't wait to see her come down those stairs.

As she starts to come down the stairs my eyes become moist, my heart was beating as I anticipated holding my sweet daughter for the first time in almost seven months. I reached out to her and she reached out to me as we embraced with the hug of a lifetime. As I am writing this, tears are strolling down my face as I remember the moment when time stood still and I just held my beautiful daughter. I didn't want to let go, I just wanted to stay in this moment forever. I'm thinking of a song by Aerosmith that says, "I don't want to close my eyes, I don't want to fall asleep because I'll miss you babe and I don't want to miss a thing!" I'd already missed the last seven months and I didn't want to miss anymore of Sabrina's life. I love you Sabrina and I am sorry for everything.

Before the blowup my relationship with Sabrina went beyond special, it was spectacular. We had so much in common, our personalities, our humor; we just had an easy, fun relationship. I'm thinking of the time when she was in junior high school and she just finished a track meet, where, as usual she did awesome. I let her drive home from the track meet when she was only fourteen years old. That was fun, but not too smart.

While I was holding Sabrina I was thinking that if I could have I would have taken a big mental and emotional eraser and wiped away the previous seven months from all of our memories. I still wish it never would have happened. I feel like such a pansy as I can't seem to stop the tears from rolling down my face as I remember the way things used to be. (Can you hear the song playing...? Memories of the way we were)

As we drove Sabrina back to our house I couldn't help but notice how beautiful and peaceful she looked. When we arrived at our humble abode Sabrina ran out of the car and into the house where she and Ellen let out a simultaneous yell of joy. It was joy unspeakable and full of glory! We all then met in the kitchen and got caught up on what was transpiring in each of our lives. Ellen then looked at Sabrina's body and said, "Oh my God , your boobs are bigger than mine!" (awkward)

The next morning I woke Sabrina up and off we went to spend some quality time together. I took her to Vanity Tan where we both got a tan and some more wrinkles. We were going to my niece's wedding that night downtown, so we had to look our best. We then sat at McDonalds and ate together and chit chatted. This is where she informed me that while she was at the Shelter of Love that she went to see a counselor. I've come to find out that he's not certified. This is when Sabrina surprisingly told me that this counselor in 30 minutes found out exactly what was wrong with her and that she's never seen him since. Wow! I didn't think 30 minutes was long enough to even tell the story of the collapse of our home, but what do I know?

That night we went to the The Hilton Hotel where we witnessed a beautiful ceremony where my niece was united together with the man of her dreams. It was a very festive evening involving music, dancing and some really good eats. (As we say in Oklahoma). My dad told me while he and Sabrina talked that she told him how much she loved and respected me and that I was her favorite person on the earth. My Dad thought to himself, Why then have you drug him through all this mud?

Sabrina would now begin coming home on the weekends until school was out in June. I talked with Lester and he thought Sabrina was ready to come back to our house on a full time basis. Were we ready for the adjustment? Could Ellen resist the temptation to be Sabrina's savior? On the 1st of June Sabrina came back home and we welcomed her with open arms of love. It had been a long journey, but we were so glad our darling daughter was finally reunited with us. (Reunited and it feels so good….)

Chapter 14

She's Baaack!

Sabrina was now back in the family fold and ready to be a big contributor to the love, joy and respect that our family once had. The hurt was behind us and we now had a great testimony of how we were all able to overcome the pain of the past and move together as one cohesive family unit. Ellen knew her place as a sister and not a caretaker and Sabrina knew her important role of being the sweet girl she was her first 15 years in our home and Sarah and I were prepared make the next three years the greatest years Sabrina had ever experienced! We were experiencing the sweet smell of restoration in all of our lives. Welcome home, our loving, youngest daughter, we love you now and always will!

It was an absolute pleasure having Sabrina back in our house again. To hear her loud laugh, her funny humor and most of all her great personality, it was a dream come true to have her home. She had even begun to help out around the house, by picking up her clothes, doing the dishes or contributing in many other thoughtful and caring ways. Wow! Life couldn't be better.

Sabrina had been home nine days when she went to her mother and asked, "Mom, can I go to the movies with all my new friends from the Christian school?" Sarah quickly answered, "You bet sweetheart, do you need me to drive you?" Sabrina said that she didn't need a ride and that her friends were coming over to pick her up. It was a Sunday night when all this took place, a day in which I'm tired from working all weekend.

When I arrived at our home on this particular Sunday night I just wanted to give my precious wife the gift I had gotten for her and hunker down for a good, restful nap. A friend who I work with had made my wife some homemade soap and shower gel and I was delivering the goods to my beautiful wife. She loves little, thoughtful presents like this, it doesn't take much to satisfy the woman of my dreams.

Before I could lie down and start my much needed nap to refresh my tired body Sabrina walks in the bedroom and says, "Dad, do you want to come meet all my new friends?" I replied,"Sabrina, I'm very tired from the work week can I meet them later?" She gave me a really disappointed look that I wasn't doing what she asked me to do.

As my loving wife was walking Sabrina out the door Sabrina stopped dead in her tracks, turned around to my wife and brazenly said, "What's wrong with Dad? Why won't he come meet my friends? Did I do something wrong, again?" Sarah responded, "Sabrina, Dad loves you, he's just tired."

Off Sabrina went to the movies with her new Christian friends to enjoy some good, exciting fellowship. Sarah informed me of Sabrina's insecure feelings concerning me not meeting her friends when she asked me to. I told Sarah that we were going to nip that type of communication in the bud and sit Sabrina down and tell her we love her, but that type of communication is very deceptive and won't be tolerated. I don't know where she learned to go to everybody except the person she has a problem with? The good book says if you have a problem with your brother go to him and talk to him first. Sabrina somehow had a built-in mechanism to tell everybody else, except the person she was currently having a problem with how she felt.

Before Sabrina arrived back at the house after going to the movies Sarah and I prayed that Sabrina wouldn't be offended at our correction and that we would all have grace to deal with this situation. As we began to talk to Sabrina she abruptly interrupted us and cut us off mid-sentence and said, "You guys are supposed to listen to me, and I want to let ya'll know that I think you guys are horrible Christian parents!" Sarah, not wanting World War II grabbed Sabrina by the hand and compassionately began trying to reason with Sabrina. This seemed to empower Sabrina as she began doing the exact opposite of everything we asked her to do. If we said sit down then she stood up or vice versa.

The monster within Sabrina was back on the prowl and man was she going to roar this time. She would take no prisoners!

I told Sabrina to shut her d… mouth and go to her room. When she got to her bedroom door it sounded like an earthquake hit the house as Sabrina almost kicked the door off its hinges. (Wham!) I looked at my wife and said, "Who does she think she is kicking the doors in our house?" I headed down the hall as my wife was grabbing my arm, trying to restrain me from falling prey to Sabrina's desire to be the victim. As I walked into the room Sabrina took two steps towards me (about 6 inches from my grill) and said in a deep voice, "What are you going to do big boy?" I restrained myself from doing what Sabrina wanted me to do and said, "Sabrina, I'm calling the director of the Shelter of Love and I'll bring you the phone and let you talk to him!"

My wife and I informed Lester of Sabrina's behavior and he was in total shock. He even said that he was speechless because she was such an angel to them for the 6 months they had her. He asked if he could talk to his former little disciple.   As I walked into the room I was not ready for what I was about to behold. There Sabrina was sitting on the ground with her legs crossed with a Bible on her lap waiting for me to bring the phone to her with Lester on the other end. When I handed her the phone she spoke to Lester in a little baby voice and said, "Lester, would you pray with me, my Dad cursed at me." She then began crying as Lester took the bait to rescue this poor hurting child from her abusive father. I'll give Lester credit; it took Sabrina over 6 months to begin pulling the wool over his eyes.

I am still amazed how Sabrina's countenance goes from Mike Tyson to a Tinker bell look so quickly. I was starting to believe that all this behavior from Sabrina was an ingrained involuntary response mechanism and that she wasn't deliberately causing such division and strife. It was part of who she had become.

That night my wife and I were so disappointed that Sabrina could not stay at our home because of her lack of self-control. I drove her back to the Shelter of Love where Lester and Betsy could handle the little bucking bronco better than us. On the way out to the compound I tried to encourage Sabrina that she was a great girl and we were good parents, but it just wasn't a good fit for all of us at this time.

I helped Sabrina bring in her belongings and gave her hug and said, "I love you and I'm sorry it didn't work out." Before I left Lester walked me out to my car where he gave me some advice. He said, "Kevin, I've learned you can never curse at a woman, never." Lester had taken the bait and was now viewing Sabrina as the victim that she so desperately wanted to be. I told him that nobody was getting in my grill without some type of repercussions. Good bye Lester! I don't think the 30 minutes of counseling Sabrina received from the unlicensed counselor was as effective as everyone had hoped. Here comes the fun part of the whole story. Now we will see how a Christian ministry begins to

enable and rescue our poor, deranged daughter. Hold onto your seat as the roller coaster ride really begins to take some sudden turns involving the courts, child support, lies from Lester and so on and so forth…..
(WEE!)

Chapter 15

The Art of Deception

Sarah and I were in total shock as to how Sabrina could take our family and after all we've been through, just flush us right down the proverbial toilet. By Sabrina's actions she was saying that she had just taken a huge crap named Mom and Dad and put her hand on the lever and away goes Mom and Dad down the drain. She then stands up and says, "Have a nice ride Mom and Dad, I hope you enjoy the smell while I'm at my Christian school, and Christian girl's home, enjoying all my Christian friends." She then smiles and smirks and let's out a sinister tirade that says, "Good luck, Mom and Pops, we'll see who has the last laugh." (HA HA HA)

This would be a turning point in our relationship with the Shelter of Love and Sabrina and you'll soon see that it will also involve Ellen the "enabler". You'll see first hand how Lester and Betsy will begin viewing Sabrina as their "prize possession' and exploiting her for financial gain. All the help we used to give her in school, all the times we took her to select sporting teams, all the times we took her to church to lay a foundation in her life, Lester and Betsy would now take the credit as the rescuing team that leads Sabrina to the light.

We had no contact with Sabrina for the next three months. There was the usual peace in our home that had been there the last two decades, minus the blip on the radar screen that Sabrina caused. That's when the phone rings and sure enough it's the Shelter of Love. I answered the phone and said, "Hello." It's Lester on the other end and he begins to explain that he's being investigated by the State of Oklahoma because he has girls older than 18 years old still living with him. Why would girls want to stay in his house so long? Why was he the only alpha male in the house? Were we headed down the path of another Waco compound?

"Kevin, the State of Oklahoma is requiring that if I want to remain a 501c3 organization, and not be under State regulation that every parent must go through the courts and write me in as managing conservator over their child." I stopped him and responded, "Lester, I know Sabrina does better with you guys than in our house but I don't want to give up any parental rights that I currently have." He comforted me with compelling words indicating that the exact same agreement we always had is the same one that will exist, the only difference is that the paperwork will be submitted through the court system. The agreement we had was basically that if Sabrina had to go to the doctor or dentist that Lester could take her. (Not Lester, but Betsy would take Sabrina because Lester's legally blind and can't operate a motor vehicle). This girl's home was Lester's only way to earn money now that his eyesight was waning, but I'm sure that has nothing to do with Lester's desire to keep every child he can for financial gain and especially his new prize possession. (Sabrina)

Lester asked if Sarah and I would drive out to the compound and sign the papers within the next week. I talked it over with my wife and since we couldn't allow Sabrina to slice and dice us up like shredded cheese anymore we decided to keep her out at the compound. The next day we drove out to the compound where Lester was waiting for us with open, loving and sincere arms. (And a pen to make sure we signed on the dotted line!)

We all talked and chit chatted about Sabrina as Lester informed us of how much Sabrina missed us and wanted to see us. He walked us to her room and showed us where she now lay her head down at night, etc... I told Lester that it was just nice having a break from all the DRAMA. We then sat down at his kitchen table and Lester pulled out the pen and handed it to me and Sarah. He then welled up with tears and began to look sad as he told Sarah and I, "Kevin and Sarah, I wish to God that you and Sabrina had contact, I know she misses her mother and father." Was Lester sincere or was he using the skillful art of deception to get us to sign those papers and then run to the courts hoping for child support? Did he really want us to see Sabrina or was Lester manipulating us until the ink was dry on the new contract? We signed the papers, not knowing the true intent and motive of Lester's heart and how he planned to steal, kill and destroy from our once happy American family. (Lester wanted to be the new "DADDY").

We left the Shelter of Love and carried on with our normal routine until the month of November. We were currently assisting our good friends, who were pastors in Norman by helping them with their children's ministry. We seem to have a gift for making church fun for kids around the ages of 6 – 12 years old. In spite of Sabrina's attempt to negatively influence as many people as she could against us, we still prodded on and tried to take our eyes off our own troubles and focus on helping others.

This particular day we were driving around to local restaurants and asking for free donations to give to the under privileged kids at the church. It's amazing how a free lunch or a surprise can light up a child's heart and make them feel special! As we were driving around Sarah and

I had the thought of what Lester said to us the last time we met when we signed the papers giving him managing conservator ship over Sabrina. We recalled the tears and the pain in his emotions when he said, "I wish to God that you had some type of communication with your daughter!" Did he really mean this or did he believe that since Sabrina was so good for him that we were to blame for her insubordination and haughty rebellious attitude?

We decided to drive to Sabrina's Christian school and say hello to our troubled daughter. Why do we keep trying to express our love for our youngest daughter? You who are parents know that no matter the pain and struggles you go through your love never changes for your child. Am I right? As we walk up to the administration office and request to see Sabrina the secretary gets up and walks to the back and talks to the principal. Here's what she says, "Dear principal, you'll never guess who's here to see Sabrina Bassoon, her parents." He is shocked and immediately informs the secretary to call Lester and tell him that we were at the school trying to see our daughter whom we still had parental rights over.

The principal walks outside with the biggest ear to ear smile and says, "Mr. Bassoon what a pleasure to finally meet you, you have the most unbelievably precious daughter in the whole world." He then says what a coincidence but Lester Mulligan from the Shelter of Love is on the phone and wants to talk to you. I was a little confused, all we wanted to do was say hi to Sabrina and leave the premises. We were hoping that even though Sabrina couldn't live with us she could at least know that we still loved her!

I picked up the phone and I sure as hell wasn't ready for the way Lester was fixing to respond. Here's what he said, "Kevin, what are you doing at the school without my permission? You know this will be too hard on Sabrina's emotions without me being there to help her. She's been through so much and I as her new managing conservator need to be there to uphold my God given daughter!" What a change since we signed he papers to be submitted to the courts? Lester was no longer a mediator, he officially saw himself as the new adopted Father of this poor, innocent, sweet angel. Lester loved Sabrina more than me or her mother.

I hung up the phone and drove off the premises and called Lester on his cell phone. I said, "Lester who the hell do you think you are telling me when, where or how I will see my daughter?" He said, "Kevin there has just been a big problem with terrorists blowing up schools and I just wanted to make all the necessary precautions that we didn't have another Columbine in Norman, Oklahoma." I think you can see where this story is headed. Lester was now comparing me to a terrorist when only 2 months before he was in tears about me and my wife having more contact with Sabrina. Why the change Lester? Was I the only dad who Lester would begin opposing? Or would there be another dad who had to go with armed officers to the compound to retrieve his wayward daughter?

Here's an excerpt from the last newsletter regarding this father who had the balls to extradite his daughter from David Koresh Jr.'s compound. This is Lester's interpretation of what happened: Later on, after having problems with her dad, the mother called us to come get her since her dad again told her to leave. We talked to her step mom to confirm what she said and she said yes, it was true and it would be better if the girl lived with us. The next day the dad took a police officer to the school to get her. When she wasn't there he came to our home and made her go home with him. Lester then belittles the authority figure all the while making himself sound like the POPE looking down on this poor, deceived father. Lester must have thought, "Shoot, there goes 20% of that man's salary right through my fingertips, son of a biscuit eater!"

Later that day I left a message on the Shelter of Love answering machine telling Sabrina that we heard she was doing good in sports and that we loved her. She called back and left a message saying, "Dad, thanks for calling, I hope you and Mom are doing well and ya'll have a great Thanksgiving!"

What should we do? We didn't want our daughter going into foster care, nor did we want her drinking Lester's kool-aid of "brainwashing". This road is fixing to get more slippery than the original slip and slide. The lines are being drawn in the sand and Lester's starting to hunker down in his fox hole! He now views himself as an assigned messenger from God to deliver kids from the authority figures in their life and re-write himself in as their new GOD-GIVEN DADDY, Daddy Lester. We then read some of Lester's newsletters and found these interesting characteristics: exaggerations, manipulation, a spiritual persecution complex with those who disagree with him, and character assassination veiled with, "Please pray for...."

I'll leave you with another excerpt from Lester's January 2005 newsletter: The hidden culture of child abuse where predators disguised themselves as parents or guardians or caretakers abandoned their defenseless daughters to a life of pain and suffering: a life that would require years of confronting the hurt while wrongfully wondering what they did wrong. Innocence? It was lost on a day when someone lustfully put their selfish, sinful desires ahead of an innocent child's well-being.

I know you're reading this and thinking what else could go wrong on this twisted road of dysfunctional relationships? My answer to you is that there's a whole lot more dung left to spread around, so hold onto your seats and get ready to witness the director of the girl's home caught in many lies and deceptions! Should I already give away the fact that his wife has never had a relationship with her father? No, I won't give away anymore tidbits of info, you'll have to read on.

CHAPTER 16

Ellen Is Re-Recruited

Ellen, my eldest daughter had been attending college on a volleyball scholarship. She seemed to be doing well academically, socially and definitely excelling in sports. She had been set free from the cobwebs that bound her soul through the manipulation of her baby sister and was heading in the right direction of growing up emotionally.

We were providing her with a nice car, paying her car insurance, her cell phone, paying on all 4 of her credit cards and also paying off her $1200.00 dental bill. When we could we would travel down to the city where she was attending college and watch her play volleyball and after the games would have dinner with her and buy her some groceries. I was so happy that she was developing new relationships and leaving her baby sister alone liked we asked so Sabrina could learn independence and mature a little emotionally.

Little did we know that Ellen was not doing what we asked, but was secretly calling Sabrina at nighttime with the cell phone we provided to check up on her baby sister? For some reason Ellen didn't do us the courtesy of asking us what we thought about her relationship with

Sabrina. She decided enough time had elapsed and Sabrina and her didn't have the problems we thought they did. Why would a college athlete be more concerned about her sister than enjoying the freedom of college? Did I mention to you that Ellen and Sabrina are co-dependant. They don't see themselves as separate entities, they view themselves as one united unit, like Siamese twins. United we stand, divided we fall!

I called Ellen and informed her of the compelling drama arising again regarding Lester and the Shelter of love and them not wanting us to see Sabrina without Lester's abiding presence. That is when she threw me another curveball. I was always a better fastball hitter in baseball, these deceptive, manipulative rescuing games I'm just not good at. I do better with right to the point, direct communication, but that's not what I was getting from the Christian ministry, Ellen or anyone else that had a heightened since of estrogen.

As I told Ellen of the resurfacing issues at hand, that's when she stopped me and said, "Dad, I've been talking to Sabrina on a consistent basis without you're knowledge and out of no disrespect for you I would like to inform you that Sabrina has been completely healed by JESUS from all previous problems." She proceeded, "Dad, I've never seen another human that loves JESUS like my sister, when I talk to her I just glean from her relationship with THE KING!" (Where the hell is the kool-aid?)

I told Ellen I don't give a darn what she in her 19 year old mind thinks regarding her sisters spiritual condition, if she continued to talk to her sister and didn't remove her co-dependant self from the picture that she was going to have some new responsibilities on her hand, like a car payment, a cell phone payment, a dental bill and a some new credit card payments! Ellen's answer was, "I'll pray about what I'm supposed to do?" Ellen is better at religious manipulation and Sabrina is better at emotional manipulation, wow, what a TEAM. You have to know your gifts.

The next morning I was at Ellen's college ready to confiscate everything I was currently paying for and let her learn some newfound responsibility. As I arrived in town I called Ellen and as she answered I said, "Hello, honey, can you come downstairs and empty your car out and give me your cell phone and I'll hand you your dental bill for $1200.00?" She came downstairs and looked totally shaken. I hugged her and said,"I love you" and drove off with my new car.

Is that too hard for you readers? I'm sure now days it's a very rare occurrence for a dad to call their children's bluff. It would be more acceptable in today's society to negotiate and find a middle ground whereby both parties are pleased with the outcome. I'm pleased and proud to say that in my life it's non-negotiable regarding my children's defiance of my authority. (even if that defiance is covered up with religiosity). I'm not as concerned with my approval rating as some spineless parents are in today's society. Just think if Rosie, Hillary or Oprah had a dad that stood their ground and said, "You can't manipulate me even if you try to make me a gelding in front of the whole world." Those sweet little "MEN HATERS" might have been corralled back down to planet earth. (Don't shout me down when I'm preaching good!)

What do you think Ellen's response was? Would it be one of personal responsibility or do you think she might be tempted to call the Shelter of Love and paint herself as the victim and attempt to have them rescue her from the certain doom of PERSONAL RESPONSIBILITY? You got it right, Ellen informed the compound where Sabrina was that she had no more transportation and was abandoned by the same parents that forsook Sabrina. That's when Lester and Betsy put their plan of rescuing our second daughter into high gear and gave Ellen a truck that was donated to the ministry. They are a 501c3 organization so they can take ministry funds or donations to use them however JESUS leads them, unhindered by any GOVERNMENT regulation. No wonder they refused to come under the licensing of the State of Oklahoma, they don't have to submit to the FEDERAL GOVERNMENT when they're submitted to JESUS! (SCARY!)

I knew then that Lester and Betsy would take my daughters' previous rebellion to an even higher level and show them how to usurp our authority, rescue and control all under the name of MINSTRY! If Liza Montana showed the girls how to drive a train of destruction through our once happy home, the Shelter of Love would show the girls how to fly a 747 of destruction right through our AMERICAN FAMILY!

I envision Betsy buckling Ellen and Sabrina into their seats as Lester is starting up the 747 that's camouflaged with the word "MINISTRY" on the side so no one can detect the heavy payload they can drop on functional homes. Betsy sits down next to Lester and puts her seatbelt on and turns on the microphone and excitedly says, "My God given daughters, I'm about to teach you through my personal experience of never having a relationship with my dad how to steal, kill and destroy the very ones God says to honor and respect all the days of your life." Ellen and Sabrina look at each other and begin clapping and saying, "Bring on the deception, this is good stuff MOMMA AND DADDY."

Lester grabs the microphone and says, "My darling GOD GIVEN daughters don't leave me out of all the fun, I'm a pretty good rescuer myself." He reminds the girls that as the only male around to just look at the way he always disagrees with the father figures and demonizes them and makes himself look superior. All the girls begin clapping and say, "Les-ter , Les-ter, Les-ter."

Lester and Betsy take off and put the plane on idle and go back and hug the girls and tell them, "We'll never leave you and never forsake you like your no good parents." They all close their eyes and begin humming and repeating over and over again , "Let the brainwashing begin, let the brainwashing begin….."

CHAPTER 17

Lies, Lies, Lies and More Lies!

The last time we talked to Sabrina was around Thanksgiving when she returned my call and left the sweetest, upbeat message saying that she loved us and hoped all was well with her old parental figures. Would Ellen's re-recruitment empower Sabrina to re-think her reconciliatory call, and would she rejoin forces with Ellen to steal, kill and destroy from her parents once again? Would they go back to the familiar co-dependant team of Ellen and Sabrina? (Till death do us part)

It had been approximately six months since we'd seen Sabrina so we decided to surprise her at one of her home basketball games. My good friend Van, my son Michael and his wife, and Sarah and I planned a surprise visit to the Christian school to watch our athletically gifted daughter lead her team to victory. The game was scheduled at 7 p.m. on a Tuesday night. All of us met at the Chili's restaurant in town and had a good time of fellowship before we piled into my friends SUV and drove to the Christian school.

We failed to inform Lester and the David Koresh, Jr. compound that we were coming without their permission to see our daughter play hoops. Lester hates it when he doesn't know exactly when, where or how there will be a meeting between parents and any of his 'GOD-GIVEN" daughters. Webster's defines control as: to exercise restraining or directing influence over, to regulate. It also says it is to exercise power over; to rule! King Lester was now in control over Sabrina's soul and we were being x'd out by Daddy Lester. (We quit giving him money and noticed a 180 degree change!)

When we arrived at the gym that night there were seven armed U.S. Marshals waiting for us...... (I'm kidding, I'm kidding). Actually, when we walked into the gymnasium there were only a token few people there. The game had been cancelled due to the other team not showing up. Our desire to see Sabrina was thwarted again. That's when Van said, "Let's drive out to the compound and surprise them, so I can see Sabrina." My buddy has been around our family for over 12 years and couldn't believe the downward spiral Sabrina had taken. He knew Sabrina when she was only 4 years old. Did Sabrina still remember him or his family, did she remember her old aunts, uncles or cousins from her 'past life?" We were thinking of bringing pictures and showing her what a great life she use to have. But we knew Lester would have none of that. His brainwashing was going as planned and nobody would thwart all the effort he and Betsy had put into their prize possession! (She's one hell of a fundraising tool)

We all climbed into the SUV and were driving out to the compound. On the way we discussed the possible scenarios of what might happen. Could we just enter the gated compound and sit down and say hello to Sabrina and catch up on old times or would Lester's defense mechanism kick in and he escort us violently off his property? I'm getting excited thinking about it and I already know the outcome.

It was a pitch black night when we entered the compound and started slowly driving to the front of the house. There are lots of trees protecting the house from the outside world. As we stopped the car in the front of the house and turned off the engine there was total quietness as we all walked to the front door, unannounced? Before we knocked on the front door I peered through an opening in the window and saw a bunch of girls sitting around Lester gleaning from his WISDOM. (Did I mention he's the only alpha male in the house?)

I lifted up my hand and knocked on the huge front door. (KNOCK, KNOCK, KNOCK)

I saw Sabrina jump up from the table and sprint to the back of the house. Did they have an escape plan ready in case we, like the other dad was brazen enough to come get one of Lester's GOD-Given daughters? Lester opened the front door and looked startled as he said, "Kevin, I've been advised by my attorney not to allow you or your family to even see your daughter!"

I looked like a deer in headlights as I said nothing. My son on the other hand spouted out, "I'm her brother, am I allowed to see her with your permission?" Lester said, "NO" and shut the door. Why was Ellen allowed to see and talk to Sabrina but not her brother? Was it a girls' only sleepover and no men were allowed except Lester? Was Lester playing late night sneaky, sneaky or was he just being a great spiritual protector from all the evil trying to attack his new daughter (formerly known as my daughter)?

We all got back into my friends' SUV and drove back to Chili's where we sat down and ate a little food and pondered over the new drama involving Sabrina. When Sabrina left Shawnee the strife and division immediately halted. Now that she's in Norman the hornet's nest has followed her out to her new location. Is she infected with the STRIFE virus? Does she attract rescuers and defenders that easily? I see Lester and Betsy, the Christian school, Ellen and her christian friends pushing Sabrina around in a wheel chair as she is bandaged from head to toe with the pain of her past! It's good to have people in her life that take care of her, unlike her no good evil parents who believe in personal accountability. (The lines are being drawn in the sand)

The next day I called Lester's legal representative who goes to the same church as Lester and said, "Elizabeth, did you inform your client not to allow me to see my child whom I still have parental rights? I also pulled out our legal agreement and read to her how that several sections of our agreement had been violated through Lester's controlling behavior." I was shocked to hear her response. She said, "Kevin, I'm sorry to tell you that Lester misrepresented what I said and basically lied using my name." For a lawyer to admit their client would resort to lying to get their way was amazing! This Director of a Christian compound was willing to lie to protect his God- given daughter. Lester really did love Sabrina in a very, very special way. (SINNER!)

The night we were refused the right to see our little bucking bronco, Sabrina called us on the telephone. It's the first contact we'd had with her since she left that sweet, thoughtful message at Thanksgiving time. I looked at caller ID and sure enough it's Sabrina calling from the compound. I answered the phone and we made a little small talk, until Sabrina revealed the real reason of her call. Her voice changed to that of Mike Tyson as I also heard someone pick up on the other end of the phone to witness every single word that would be spoken. Sabrina said, "Dad, why do you want to see me now, I thought you said youngest daughters are controlling and manipulative? Don't you think all this contact will be too hard for my emotions?" I tried to slowly, thoughtfully interject some calm words as Sabrina seemed to be pulling me, challenging me to lose my temper and thus justify herself with whoever was sneakily listening on the other end of the phone line. Sabrina then abruptly says, "Dad, you sound really angry, are you angry dad? I didn't hear you Dad, I said, are you angry? Huh?"

I handed the phone to my wife to give myself a break from the severe emotional manipulation of my youngest daughter. That's when Sabrina told her mother, "I don't want to see ya'll for a long time" and hung up the phone in the lady's ear who 16 years before gave birth to her in a hospital room in Tulsa, Oklahoma. (Lester and Betsy's mind control was starting to bear fruit)

When my son heard about Sabrina's disrespectful attitude towards me and his mother   he immediately called his baby sister and said, "You're a liar, Sabrina, you've lied about the way our family is, you lied about Dad hitting you, and you're not ever going to see my baby if you don't change the crooked path you're on!!!" She responded not with the Mike Tyson voice she had with me, but she went to the more effective Tinker bell voice and began weeping as the Directors of the compound, her Christian friends and Ellen all began hugging her and praying for the deliverance of her soul from the attacks of her former "FAMILY". (In the name of Jesus this house is now –CLEAN!)

Sabrina called Michael back later in the week to see if he could be re-recruited back on Ellen's and her new team. She got a reality check that Michael was through with all the teenage drama and was more interested in being a good father and husband. I'm so glad Michael and his beloved bride got to see firsthand the incident at he compound so they could understand for themselves what a sick, controlling place Sabrina was now in! (You shall know the truth and the truth shall set you free.)

It's now getting close to Christmas time and there are some new interesting developments on the horizon concerning Ellen, Sabrina, the girl's home and our Pastors. Our good friends, who are pastors, are going to make a surprise visit to the compound and experience first hand the controlling, deceptive behavior of Lester and Betsy. The lights are being turned on and the darkness is being exposed. Would this make Lester and Betsy see the light and turn the other direction or would they hunker further down in their foxhole of deception and take on all wise counsel and resist the truth, vehemently? Read on and you shall be surprised at what happens next!

CHAPTER 18

Is This a Cult?

Webster defines a cult as: a great devotion to a person, idea, object, movement, or work. It also says it is a small group of people characterized by such devotion. A cult always appears on the outside to be walking in the light, until you look deep into the motivations of the leaders and realize all the honor and worship are really aimed at the "WISE LEADERS". (David Koresh)

I was starting to finally add some things up regarding the interior operations of the Shelter of Love and began pondering these seven things:

I.   There was no licensed counselor and no affiliation with the State of Oklahoma.

II. They consistently usurped parents' authority. (there are no pictures of any happy parents on their website)

III. They had a viewpoint that the world was evil. (boycotted certain businesses for religious reasons)

IV. The leaders had no kids of their own. (only God-Given daughters)

V. Lester was the only male around all these teen-age girls.

VI. Their website showed testimonies of girls exalting Lester as the new father figure in their lives ,while degrading the paternal parents. (I like the one with Lester walking a girl down the aisle on her wedding day)

VII. The longer the girls stay at the compound they have less and less contact with the outside world, including family.

Since Lester was now lying to me and my family on a consistent basis and had become public defender #1 for my daughters, and his attorney also implied to me that the judge presiding over the managing conservator ship was requesting 20% of my salary, I knew it was time to hire an attorney. I opened the local yellow pages and found someone who practiced family law named Perry Tisdale. I immediately called and set up an appointment for11 a.m. on a Friday morning.

I arrived at Perry Tisdale's office at 10:45 and made some small talk with his legal secretary. We were about the same age and she also was experiencing the challenges of raising teenagers in today's society. As I began to open up about the problems we were currently facing with our rebellious daughters being empowered by a Christian girl's home I mentioned the names Lester and Betsy Mulligan. This lady stopped me mid-sentence as her jaw hit the floor like a skydiver freefalling from the sky and said, "Who did you say?" I replied, "Lester and Betsy Mulligan of The Shelter of Love."

Her eyes almost bugged out of her cranium as she said, "My God that's the same place Perry took his daughter to and had some unbelievable problems, just like you're having!" Wow! What a coincidence, the one lawyer I picked out of the yellow pages and he too had suffered at the hands of the same Christian ministry as me and my wife. Were we uncovering the operations of a cult that operates under the disguise of the word MINISTRY? I couldn't wait until the attorney arrived so we could trade stories of the collapse of our American families and the covert operations of the girl's home.

When the aforementioned attorney walked into the room his legal secretary mentioned that I was his eleven o'clock appointment and that I was having some difficulty with Lester and Betsy Williams. His head immediately shot upward and said, "Please come into my office and have a seat."

Perry began courageously telling me of the pain of his past as an American Dad and all the troubles his daughter went through before he had no other choice but to put her into the deceitful hands of the Shelter of Love. This attorney suffers from severe physical handicaps and has trouble even walking. He told me his daughter use to hit him and that he could barely defend himself because of his handicap. I was shocked to hear that Lester told him the problem was that he was too easy on his daughter and needed to toughen it up. Ouch!

I was starting to get the picture, Lester always disagrees with the authority figure and ends up rescuing the teenage girl and therefore forms an emotional allegiance with these rebellious, angry teenage girls. He villianizes the parents and comforts and agrees with the girls to win their love, approval and most of all their lifelong commitment to him, THE LEADER! Is this brainwashing or what?

The deception in which this Christian girl's home was operating in was to a degree that I had only seen and heard about at the Waco, Texas compound led by the now deceased David Koresh. Webster's defines deception as: double dealing suggests treachery or at least action contrary to a professed attitude (a go between suspected of double dealing). Lester was representing himself and ministry to the outside world as a thoughtful, caring rehabilitative refuge for families, when in fact Lester was double dealing towards hurting parents by betraying trusts and confidences to steal, kill and destroy from the very fabric of the family. The outside glamour wasn't matching the inside tactics that Lester was now operating in. I don't think Lester started out this way but obviously something changed and Lester was now becoming the ultimate wedge between families and their reconciliation process.

Back to the office visit with the attorney who was divulging some serious incriminating evidence into the operations of the Shelter of Love. He confided in me that it would be extremely hard for him to take this case due to a conflict of interest. He told me he went to the same church as Lester and his attorney and that if he was called to the witness stand that he'd have to divulge the truth and that his relationship with Lester and Betsy would be destroyed forever and be unrepairable. He looked hesitant, very hesitant to go after this hornet's nest of a problem and uncover the darkness that existed at the compound. (Little Waco)

That's when he opened up and told me this, "Kevin, my daughter is in college now and has nothing to do with me, even though she now loves Lester and Betsy just like she once loved me." He looked sad, and I understood his emotions, for I too have experienced the same pain as he did. Maybe for that one day it was just good for me to listen to him and him to listen to me as we both comforted each other as two American Dads in a changing society.

As I was walking to my car after the enlightening appointment my mind did a flashback to a letter the Shelter of Love wrote to me and my lovely bride when in their unlicensed opinion they perceived that our daughter was completely healed and ready to return to our house after receiving thirty minutes of intensive psychotherapy counseling. Here are some of the excerpts from the letter dated May 24, 2006:

Kevin and Sarah,

You can certainly be proud of the way Sabrina is allowing GOD to work in her life! It would be a shame if she couldn't go back to the Christian school. The school is an excellent Bible-based school and solves the problem of putting her back into GOVERNMENT schools.

In fact we hate to LOSE Sabrina, but our job is done here. We would however, like to KIDNAP her occasionally as we have grown to love her very much.

This letter is the last communication Lester and Betsy sent me and my family. We've never been invited to a sporting event, never been sent progress reports and never received any information on how Lester's new God-given daughter is doing. Maybe it's just a coincidence that in Lester's letter he uses the word "kidnap", and the phrase "he hates to lose Sabrina", or maybe he is running a bonafide Waco, Jr. Compound?

Could this road we're on be headed for another slippery turn? Will Lester and Betsy be confronted with the cold hard facts of their inappropriate relationships with teenage girls? Will the veil of hypocrisy be ripped down for the entire world to see if this truly is a CULT?

CHAPTER 19

Infiltrating the Compound

Our good friends, Javier and Crystal, could hardly believe the twisted road that our once happy family had been taken down. They were surprised, not that we had an initial problem with Sabrina, because they themselves have raised 3 daughters, so they knew firsthand the power of estrogen. But they could hardly believe all the bad counsel we all received from the Swaggert's, to the Montana's, to the Pastor who hated his father and last but not least the Christian girl's home. To me the Christian girl's home was just the icing on the cake of this whole nightmare we've ALL been drug through!

I wish someone would slap me in the face and tell me this really didn't happen and that it was all just derived to make this book sound interesting. Again I'm sad to report that these tragic events actually did happen and that I don't necessarily see the light at the end of this dark tunnel.

My friend Javier has been a minister for two decades in our local community and is well respected in the church world and also the secular side of society. He's been a great softball coach and trained many a girl to be all they can be on the softball fields. He has also taught these girls how to excel in the game of life.

His fun wife Crystal is a very discerning counselor, who helps run and organize a state-run facility for girls that are in real dire straits, girls that have to be locked down or could injure themselves or others. She's also been my wife's best friend during this whole rollercoaster ride our co-dependant daughters have taken us on. Thank you Crystal for your support and encouragement to my wife!

Javier and Crystal set up an appointment to talk with Lester and Betsy and find out how they got from thinking Sabrina was prepared to come home in June and then after the blowup where she kicked our door in, to having zero communication for 6 months. How could an opinion change that quickly with no parental contact? Did Lester deduce in his unlicensed opinion that if Sabrina did so well with them and not with us that that's indicative that there's something wrong with the parents? Did he conclude that since Ellen was again co-dependently rescuing sweet Sabrina and we coldheartedly ripped the car we were paying for out from under her that Ellen and Sabrina's agreement is another strike against Mom and Dad? Did I mention that Lester is unlicensed?

It was during the Christmas holidays that Javier and Crystal drove out after much prayer to the gated compound to interject some opinions from the outside world to the directors. Would they be opened to some good advice or were they hunkering down with their teenage God-given daughters?

They arrive at the compound and are greeted by Lester, Betsy and Sabrina as they all have a seat in the large living room. They all do some small talk before the conversation turns to the real reason for the visit. Javier humbles himself and divulges that he and his daughters during their teenage years had some real issues that they all had to overcome and that through the willingness of all parties worked through it using coping skills of forgiveness and personal responsibility.

That's when Betsy piped up and said, "That must have been so very difficult for your daughters to have to go through what they did, how were they able to do that?" Javier and Crystal tried to use these moments to speak truth to these unlicensed directors in charge of the reconciliation between mothers and fathers and their daughters. They very wisely said, "Every family has issues, but you have to work through them and not stay where you were emotionally when the offense took place."

That's when I realized that, that is where Sabrina is emotionally. She's still at 15 years old and Lester and Betsy with all their help to erase the memory of mama and daddy are unable to help Sabrina confront her real feelings. That's why when we see her she has all this anger, all this rebellion, all this division. They've covered up Sabrina's real emotions with church attendance, the christian school and the isolated living at the compound but it hasn't even touched her true feelings underneath the façade of religiousity!!!!

As they were all talking guess who comes waltzing in from the back of the compound. It's none other than Ellen "the enabler" who walks in sheepishly and sits down snuggled up right next to the pride and joy of her life, Sabrina. I can just imagine how Lester and Betsy must be feeling when it was revealed that they were housing and hiding Ellen from her parents. (OOPS!) This is the first Christmas Ellen didn't call or come by to see us. Did I mention Ellen and Sabrina were co-dependant, if one is mad then the other one is also? Sabrina has been angry at us since we uncovered her deceitful communication patterns and Ellen vacillates between rescuing Sabrina and also going to college. It's probably not easy on Ellen going to college and also thinking daily about her sweet, angry sister.

Before Javier and Crystal left the compound Crysal walks over and sits right in the middle between the two Siamese twins and says, "Girls, I've known you since you were real little and if you ever want to talk, I'll always be here for you!" That's a true friend of the family!! When Crystal picked her head up Betsy was giving her the EVIL EYE about suggesting anything without her permission with her new God- given daughters. Betsy must have been thinking, I've got these girls strapped into this 747 of family destruction and you're trying to untie them (I wish you'd just get the hell out of here).

Javier and Crystal left the compound after praying and hugging everybody and leaving the girls with these words, "Girls, you know your Mom and Dad talk about you all the time and love you both very much!!!" The girls began to cry as truth for the first time was being spoken to them on the premises of the compound. I hope that those words pierced right through Lester's and Betsy's brainwashing and entered my daughters' souls and that they'll always remember the truth. WE LOVE THEM BOTH!!!!!

CHAPTER 20

Is Lester a Convicted Felon?

Crystal sat down to have lunch with Lester's sister-in-law who lives in Shawnee. They are a very well to do family that has access to lots of financial resources. As they are chit chatting over a nice lunch, Crystal begins to discuss Lester and Betsy and the way they run their compound and the perilous situation that our family now found itself in. Lester's sister-in-law looks around, leans over and whispers in Crystal's ear, "Did you know that Lester is a convicted felon who served time in a federal penitentary." Crystal responded with total shock and complete astonishment. She thought to herself, how can the state of Oklahoma allow a convicted felon to house these young impressionable teenage girls?" Crystal was totally agast concerning the new revelation of Lester's past misdeeds. She then asked her friend, "Can you tell me what he did?" Lester's sister-in-law told Crystal, "He cheated and deceived the IRS and disrespected the law concerning his taxes, he was convicted of tax evasion." She continued, "Lester and Betsy know we have money and constantly try to hit us up for their ministry needs."

When Crystal told Sarah about Lester's past being exposed, Sarah called me immediately and informed me of the situation. It was all coming together to me. Lester is a con man who uses Christianity and the word "Ministry" to con people into believing he as a bona fide minister of the Gospel. I went home and immediately emailed Lester and asked him if it was true about his previous conviction and why he did not tell the truth to parents and others about his past. What do you think Lester's reply to me was? You got it right. He said nada, nothing, no reply, he pled his fifth admendment rights.

About this time Lester sent out another newsletter and as you will see his brainwashing was progressing quite well over Sabrina's young soul. A friend at the gym gave me a copy of the Shelter of Love's newsletter and told me, "You won't believe what Lester says about your underage daugher in his newsletter."

He handed it to me and as I began to read it, my stomach began to be physically ill. I had to stop reading it and go to the bathroom and relieve myself. Lester's crap was flowing through that newsletter and through my body like an over the counter laxative!

Here is what Lester says about Sabrina's unbelievable, spectacular exploits in basketball. He said, "Sabrina took over the basketball game like no other player I have ever seen on a basketball court. She willed her team to win with the greatest performance I have ever seen, including those by the great Tracy McGrady." Lester then says a dad from the opposing team came up to me and said, "Who is that number 4, she is the most talented athelete I have ever seen. She could play basketball anywhere she wanted ." Lester stood up and proudly said, "That's my daughter!" Lester had slowly progressed from seeing Sabrina as mine and Sarah's daughter that he loved very much to Sabrina being his God-given daughter to finally after all of his grooming his very own DAUGHTER. His brainwashing was finally complete and sealed with the words, you are now my property forever. Lester then ponders Sabrina's wonderful future and envisions her reproducing for him God-given grandkids that eventually become his very own grandkids.

Can you see Lester and Betsy waiting with forceps as Sarah is giving birth and taking Sabrina and saying to us, "Kevin and Sarah, thank you so much for the sperm, the egg, the investment you made during Sabrina's childhood and adolescent years. Your work is now done. Jesus wants us to be the new and improved version of Mommy and Daddy." They hug Sarah and I and try to reach in our pocketbooks and take out some cash that they will need for her new life.

This newsletter also contained information about Ellen and Sabrina being reconciled with my wife's relatives. Sarah and I had tried to protect our kids from the spiritual deception and manipulation of her family as long as we could. Let me give you a little background concerning her relatives. They are part of a family who has an elitist view of their "Christianity". (Sound familiar to Lester and Betsy.) In the year 1997, we started noticing some real troubling and disturbing things about Sarah's dad. He disagreed with the church we all used to go to in the country called Oasis of Life Church. The original Pastor John Stephens stepped down and they put in an new pastor without Sarah's family permission. This is when Allen (Sarah's Dad) started to go off the deep end and rant and rave against this church and all the people who went there. He cut off all relationships with anyone associated with Oasis of Life Church and would not even go to town and look at those sorry, no good demon-possessed people. When we would go see Allen and Kelly, Allen would say things like, "Sarah, you know your old friend Theresa Hilly who you grew up with still goes to that church and is demon-possessed with the rest of them." Then Allen would give an angry and hateful scowl and say, "These people who I have known for over a decade are just baby christians who don't get it like I do. We will start our own group. Screw them!" (It failed in a year)

Around this time Sarah's mother Kelly started telling us some outrageous stories of her sexual desires. She was abused as a little girl and really can't connect with men, she does better with women and young girls who are in need of her counseling. She use to always give me books and tapes of how to be a good father and husband. I knew she was really saying, "Kevin, please don't be a husband like Allen is to me and most of all don't be a father like my crappy dad." (Scary, I think we are on a collision course with the Mulligans) Kelly then tells us a story of her and Allen praying for a woman in the country. Kelly says to Sarah and me, "As we were praying for this lady I had an unbelievable desire to have sex with her." (I think it is time to find some new inlaws)

We did not want our daughters hanging around with these twisted, sick people but will they now team up with Lester and Betsy and further strenghten the co-dependant bond of Ellen and Sabrina? We shall see, we shall see.

I want to give you two more reasons why Sarah and I knew her parents were very dangerous people and a threat to any healthy relationship. The first incident happened while our kids were at school and Sarah and I were snuggled up in our bed relaxing and enjoying each other's company. Suddenly and unexpectedly we heard a banging on our bedroom door. (Bang Bang Bang) All of our kids were at school and no one had a key to our house. We had an intruder in our home. Mine and Sarah's hearts started beating fast as we heard her mother's voice say, "Kevin, Sarah are y'all OK?" Her parents had broke into our house and entered the bedroom uninvited. What would you, readers do if your inlaws criminally trespassed on your property? That was it for me, right then and there I finally got it. These people are certified wackos.

Kelly peeks her head in our bedroom and says, " We haven't heard from y'all in awhile and thought someone was hurt or in the hospital." My first thought was, no, we are all fine, we are all just avoiding your flaky, craziness as long as possible.

Sarah and I were barely clothed as Sarah's mother comes and sits on the bed next to me and pulls out a notebook where she had written down things going on in the FAMILY that we weren't aware of. She started reading, "Uncle Lonny and Sharon have divorced after all these years and it's good because Lonny is a horrible husband." Allen says "Amen" and then adds, "He goes off into rages and actually pulled the phone out of the wall. Jesus just used us to rescue Sharon from Lonny and help set her free. We're instruments in our Majesty's Hands." (Sound familiar to Lester and Betsy)

I could go into more detail of my inlaws like my father-in-law having a heart attack and saying, "I saw Jesus walk in my hospital room and put his hand out and say, 'Allen, your time is not yet for I have many things for you to do for me still on earth.'"(cookoo, cookoo's nest)

CHAPTER 21

Ellen's Letter

As I opened up the mailbox to check the mail I noticed a letter from Ellen that was different than her previous letters sent to Sarah and me since Operation Division began in August of 2005. This letter had a return address on it. She had been secretly and sneakily sending letters without her address on so we couldn't find her whereabouts. (I bet she thought we might say something that disagreed with her)

I opened up the letter and began to read, Dear Mom and Dad, I've been contimplating over the last several months what unbelievable, spectacular, loving parents you were to me. You provided me with waterpark season tickets, took me on vacations, drove me to school everyday and did and said so many things that said I LOVE YOU! She then said, "I want you to be a part of my life."

As Sarah and I were pondering the thoughtful apology letter we both said to one another, "I think it's good for Ellen to be away from Sabrina, the Mulligan's and Sarah's busybody parents, the Charlatons." She sounds to be slowly developing some EMOTIONAL INDEPENDANCE. I then said to the love of my life,"Sarah, why don't you drive down and see your daughter and spend some quality time with her, just the two of you enjoying each others company and catching up on old times." Sarah smiled and excitedly said, "I miss her so much, I want her to know how special she is to me!!" Her eyes literally welled up with tears as she said, "I just have to let her know my love for her will never change!" I wiped her eyes as she looked like a racoon with her mascara running down her face like a flowing river.

Ellen called me and Sarah within the next week and said, "Mom and Dad, I love you both so much. Will you forgive me for all the hurtful things I've done to you directly and indirectly." We both simultaneously responded with, "We love you and just want to get back to a normal relationship without any meladrama involved." While on the phone Sarah asked Ellen hesitantly,"Do you think it might be ok if I came to see you??" Sarah waited anxiously not knowing if Ellen would take Sabrina's knife she used to slice her heart out of her chest and reject her again or agree to allowing her mother to come see her. There was silence as Ellen finally said ,"Sure Mom I think that would be ok." Sarah looked relieved that Ellen had given her permission to see her.

Sarah was almost giddy the next week as she prepared to go see Ellen. Everytime she'd talk to someone she'd end up saying ,"Guess who I 'm going to see next week? I'm going to see my precious Ellen!!!" One night I came into the kitchen and saw Sarah going through a box she labeled Ellen. It had all of Ellen's buttons, pins, awards and was full of precious memories Sarah had saved. I asked her,"What ya doing girl?" She said,"Do you think Ellen remembers what a good mom I was to her?" I said,"All the Mulligan's and Charlaton's brainwashing will never erase the great memories you created for your daughter Ellen, never!"

Sarah loaded up the car and headed to Nashville,Tennessee where Ellen was now going to college. The Mulligan's had usurped our authority and induced Ellen to renounce her scholarship at this secular university and led her to a spirit-filled university where Ellen could seek the Lord more. (Are you surprised the Mulligan's would usurp our God given delegated authority ? I'm not)

Sarah walks into the gym and is immediately met by Ellen's volleyball coaches. They both say to Sarah, "We're so glad to finally meet Ellen's real mother, you did a great job with her, she's a great girl." Sarah shook their hands and said, "Thanks for all you 've done for my precious daughter." Ellen was practicing when Sarah came in to the gym, but made a bee line straight to Sarah and gave her the warmest hug and said, "I've missed you, Mom." (My wife couldn't hold back the tears)

That night Ellen had to work as a night monitor. Sarah went with her and along the way my precious wife gave her a card I had hand picked for her along with some money I wanted to give her. After Ellen read it she had to go to the bathroom to regain her composure. The letter expressed my deep love for Ellen and cut right through the lies of the Mulligan's and reconfirmed what Ellen always knew, "That I loved her!"

The next morning Sarah and Ellen went to chapel together and enjoyed a great time of fellowship. They hugged each other and both of them knew that the past was behind them and that the restoration had finally come. It was awesome!

On the drive home Sarah conveyed every last detail of how her and Ellen had the time of their lives. Sarah asked me on her drive home, "Kevin, do you think I was a good Mom to Ellen?" I was shocked that my rock strong wife would even ask a question like that but Ellen's and Sabrina's attacks against her had been emotionally fierce. I quickly said, "You were and are the best Mom in the world!"

She said, "Thank you Kevin, I love you."

The next day Ellen called me and said,"Dad, did you hear what a beautiful time Mom and I had together?" I told her how much it meant to her mother and that Sarah was sooo happy to see her!!

About a month later my good buddy Van and I went to Austin to surprise Ellen at one of her volleyball games. I got to meet the coaches before the game and really liked them both. Ellen saw me and Van and started coming towards us. I stood up and hugged her and she hugged me as we both were just thrilled to see each other.

After the game Ellen was the first one out of the dressing room and actually ran to me so she could spend some time with me before she had to go back to her college. We chit-chatted about nothing and then walked hand in hand to her team bus as we said our goodbyes. I looked in her eyes as she did mine and we both knew the love was still beating in our hearts towards one another. Reunited and it feels so good, reunited cause we understood..........we both are so excited cause we're reunited!!!!

As we drove back to Shawnee my good buddy said, "You can stamp this relationship with the words RESTORED. As we drove home I couldn't quit thinking of Ellen as a little girl and then as the beautiful woman she had become.

Christmas is around the corner and Ellen's coming home. Will her newfound emotional independance be able to stand up against her sister's new arsenal of friends and family(Charlatons) who want Ellen to reject us? We shall see. We shall see.

CHAPTER 22

A Christmas Surprise

My mother called and reiterated how special it was for Ellen to see both me and her mother. My mom continued ,"Kevin, Ellen is coming to see us before Christmas and then heading to Shawnee to see you guys." This will be the first time Ellen has seen her nephew, Danny. (Our real grandson, not just God-given like Lesters)

While Ellen was with my Mom she excitedly said, "Grandma , will you help make this the best Christmas ever for my Mom and Dad?" You know this is my Mothers favorite time of year. I want it to be her best Christmas ever!!!" My mom happily told Ellen that she would help her make this a wonderful Christmas. Ellen and my mom went from department store to department store picking out the most special gifts she could for all of us. There are things about Ellen that remind me of her birth mother like buying special gifts or writing beautiful notes just to say, you are special!

Ellen had a great time with my relatives in Houston and was headed towards Shawnee to see us. This was going to be the greatest Christmas of our lives. Sarah had been purchasing so many presents for Ellen, they could hardly fit in the car.

On December 21st we started calling Ellen to set up a time for us to get together and celebrate this special Christmas, but Ellen never answered our phone calls and all our calls went straight to her voice mail. Then we were informed by friends that she was staying with a friend who lives less than a mile from our house. Did Sabrina, Lester or Sarah's loopy parents take back control of Ellen's fragile soul?

My mom started calling Ellen along with other family members but all calls went unreturned. That's when my son Michael called to talk to Ellen. He dialed her number and sure enough Ellen answered and says, "Hey, Bubby how's it going?" Michael says, "Ellen, why aren't you answering your phone and when are you coming over to see my son?" Ellen hates it when she's confronted with her indirect communcation style. She got tongue-tied and began back peddling, not knowing how to respond to Michael's direct communication.

That's when Sabrina takes the phone from Ellen and tells Ellen, "Watch this sis as I take CONTROL of this situation." Ellen looked impressed with Sabrina's boldness and gleans from the now experienced veteran's angry, divisive tone of voice. Sabrina winks at Ellen while they're sitting in the Mulligan's van at Light of the World Unity church and says, "Michael, tell your mom and dad that they will always be referred to by me as Kevin and Sarah til the day I die. Jesus gave me a new Daddy just like me." (a convicted felon). Sabrina hangs up on Michael and says to everyone in the car, "Let's sing this song together, I'm so glad Lester set me free, I'm so glad that Lester set me free, singing glory hallelujah, Lester set me free....."

Sabrina leans up to the front and says to Lester and Betsy, "I think my old emotional noose I use to control Ellen with still fits, even though she's been away from us for such a long time." They both turn to her and say, "We are so proud of you, Sabrina". Sabrina then hugs them both and whispers, "Ellen isn't as strong as me but I'll help her see YOUR LIGHT." We haven't heard or seen Ellen since the bizarre incident at Christmas. (twilight zone music playing again)

CHAPTER 23

Our Lifelines

As I was amazed and astonished at the backlash of several dysfunctional families I was equally shocked at the affirmation and encouragement we received from our "TRUE FRIENDS". Sarah and I have never been wealthy, I would say we've never been even close to wealthy, but we've always been rich with the most fantastic friends in this world! (A friend loves at all times!)

Our heads at times were barely above water while our once caring and thoughtful daughters seemed to be constantly submerging us under the water of their raging teenage emotions. But through God's grace and the help of our strong supporting friends (life preservers) we've been able to carry on and fight the good fight of faith. We, at times couldn't see the forest for the trees, but we both had a strong belief that this story isn't over and that someday there shall be a complete restoration and reconciliation! We shall see, we shall see.

I remember when Sabrina first infiltrated our home with "OPERATION DIVISION" how the waves of despair kept billowing over our once happy souls, over and over again. Yet somehow, some way, we never sank, we never gave up, and I think I know why. Our friends and family rose up with us to stand by our side and said, "You're not giving in and you're not giving up." They've kept pointing us forward saying, "Don't look back, and they'd grab us emotionally and pick us up and sure enough we'd take one step at a time." Thank you, Mom, Dad, Van, Kristy, Javier, Crystal, Mike, John, Samantha, Linda, Sonny, etc. (the list could go on and on......)

Looking back, the first person I called after my home was infiltrated after taking my first deposition was my Dad. It was dark, quiet and lonely in my car as I nervously called my Dad and waited it seemed like hours for him to pick up on the other end. (ring,ring,ring..) When he picked up the phone and said hello all my emotions flowed out of me like the torrent of a raging river (boohoo, boohoo). I couldn't speak as my Dad began saying, "What is it my son? What is it? Are you okay, can I help you, please let me help you, I've never heard you like this." After I gained composure and my tear ducts were dried up, I told my Dad of how me, an American Dad was framed and set up by my beguiling daughter. He immediately responded with these words, "I've seen you with your family all these years and I know you're a great dad and a great husband." He then said, "Kevin, I'm not there with you but you're not alone." He left me with these words from the good book. Blessed be the God and Father of our Lord Jesus who comforts us in all our pain so we can turn around and comfort others in the same way we've been comforted! Wow! Thanks Dad for being the best Dad in the whole world!

The next friend that was there for me in my garden of Gethsemane experience was my old buddy, old pal Van. When I began telling Van the dramatic events he stopped what he was doing and said, "Let's go out to the bench that's in my backyard and I want to hear everything." I told Van the suspenseful story and he listened to every last word. Van then hugged me and said, "Kevin, my kids love you, and I know that someday you're daughters will come back and realize that you and Sarah were super parents!" Van gave me hope of a better tomorrow, and I began to see the possibilities on the horizon of my relationship with my daughters. All things are possible to them that believe.

In spite of mine and my wife's mistakes we were able and still do encourage each other on a daily basis with these words, all things work together for good for our family. We haven't seen the positive outcome in our relationship with our daughters that we want , but some day I promise they'll be a sequel to this book titled "THE RESTORATION OF AN AMERICAN FAMILY".

In the midst of all the tumultuous things that have happened to our family look at some of the positive things going on right now: Ellen is doing awesome in college, making a 4.0 in her first semester, all the while playing college volleyball. She is working to help suport school costs and just made 2nd team All-American. That's good stuff!!!!!

Sabrina is an honor roll student and excelling as usual in all sporting activities. She's been team captain, made all district, All-State honors, district MVP and it looks like she's going to get a volleyball scholarship to college! That's good stuff!!!

My son Michael and his wife just had their first baby, a beautiful boy named Danny Bassoon. Sarah and I just got to keep him for the first time while both his parents worked on a Sunday night. He's so cool. I think I'm going to dig being a grandpa!!!

Weeping may endure for a night but joy comes in the morning!

Is everything perfect in our once happy family? NO! But is everything perfect in your home? How about you, readers, are your homes only considered complete when everyone is feeling hunky-dory, or can you be happy even when things are a little cockeyed? Faith is believing in something you can't see. Can you see gravity, no, but I promise you'd believe in it if you jumped off a 90 story building! I believe that someday I'll experience the warmth of my daughters love and they'll experience the warmth of my love. When? I don't know, but in the meantime I'm going to live today expecting a light at the end of this dark tunnel.

ADDENDUM

Since the completion of this book we've had some interesting developments concerning the Norman County Sherriff's office involvement investigating the Shelter of Love. Chief investigator Ken Starring informed me that he has been interviewing people that have been previously involved with the Shelter of Love and here's what he informed me concerning the investigation.

Every person who has an association with Lester and Betsy seem to have a code of silence about disclosing any information about them. He told me that although it's hard to convict someone of brainwashing that there is another avenue that is being taken by the Internal Revenue Service. They are once again on to Lester and Betsy and investigator Starring said that the IRS wouldn't disclose anything else, but that when the warrant is issued we'll know about it! (GO IRS GO)

Last but not least through the urging of Ellen one of Sabrina's old friends went to see Sabrina graduate. (we weren't invited). Her name is Lisa. Her mother took her to support Sabrina. After observing Sabrina's new outward religious behavior she asked her Mom on the way home. "Mom, is that what brainwashing is?"